LYRICAL ASSASSINS

LYRICAL ASSASSINS

50 of the Greatest Prophet Emcees

LAMONTE COLLYEAR

To order additional copies of this book, contact:
Xlibris
1-888-795-4274
www.Xlibris.com
Orders@Xlibris.com
774290

CONTENTS

ACKNOWLEDGMENTS

I did it again, I completed Book number three. I want to thank my mother Mrs. G. who is always there for me. I know I can always count on her when I need a prayer to help me with any problem I'm faced with in life. I want to thank my brother Von Sr., who provides support by being a fan of all my projects. Also, I want to thank my little nephew Von Jr. (Butter) who I know may end up playing professional baseball one day. Stay focused Butter you have the bloodlines for the Majors!

I want to thank the forever gorgeous Bianca, the future mother of my seeds. Queen B keeps me updated on new music and is always a good person to converse with about everything in life. Bianca you are truly inspirational and the most special woman I've met in a long time! I want to thank the lovely Little Mama Jay T who gives me inspiration with her interest in reading my novels. Also, I want to thank Alexcez who also keeps me updated on many of the current artists and songs. Alexcez, our time together has been very valuable. Thanks again to you all.

PREFACE

The day I heard Doug E. Fresh and Slick Rick's "The Show" was the day I became a hardcore hip hop fan. It wasn't the first hip hop song I ever heard. I have to say Kurtis Blow's "The Breaks" probably was the first followed by The Sugar Hill Gang "Rappers Delight". "The Show" was the song filled with an exuberance of charisma. The Inspector Gadget beat was used brilliantly along with Doug E. Fresh's lyrics and beatboxing and Slick Rick's rhymes and British accent. I was officially hooked. Even at a young age, I knew there would be several follow ups due to the success of the song.

I was right. After the success of "The Show" and "Ladi Dadi." There was an explosion of New York rappers ready to make their respective marks in the rap game. Rappers became extremely creative to solidify their place in the world of hip hop. These lyrical assassins were a breath of fresh air, giving young black youths something to embrace and enjoy no matter what their circumstances were in society. They accomplished this by broadcasting the ills of urban society using rhyme formats with the preciseness of a skillful surgeon operating on the minds of black youths in America. In the process of this, they entertained the masses worldwide. Lyrical Assassins "50 of the Greatest Prophet Emcees" is an illustration of paying my respect to the many great men and women who provided entertainment, knowledge, and self-love in my life. There is nothing better than listening to your favorite artist go in on a track with the feeling of a pleasurable pain. The lyrics and beat will make your head nod while you are sporting the ugliest frown on your face at the same time.

Kool Mo Dee's 2003 "There's a God on the Mic" gave me the inspiration to write this book. Kool Mo Dee is a professional rap veteran with all the knowledge to accurately describe a chronicle of the greatest emcees to ever recite lyrics on a microphone. Kool Mo Dee is an expert of all the intricacies of rap. If you want a more sophisticated breakdown of your favorite rappers, I suggest you get Kool Mo Dee's book. I'm writing from the perspective of a fan only. My illustration includes mostly rappers from the eighties and nineties. I have also included a few "millennial rappers," as I call them. Every list is debatable, so that is why I had to come up with my own favorite list of great emcees. I personally thank all of you brothers and sisters (emcees) for sharing your thoughts and knowledge to the whole world. You did this by teaching me game I was not equipped for in my circumstances of growing up as a young and confused man in America. This illustration is a way for me to express how much I appreciate the music and to give these talented individuals their well-deserved props. The brothers and sisters listed in this book helped me survive my military years and college days. They are also currently helping me get through the stressful times of the everyday work flow. Hip hop music has helped me weather the storms of some of the most challenging trials and tribulations of my life.

Anytime someone comes up with any kind of list, or ranking, there will always be room for debate. This book represents my personal favorites from number one to fifty, with a list of honorable mentions and top fifty rap groups. Let me make myself clear, it is simply my personal opinion. Once again, I want to say thanks to these prophets who gave me a reason to be happy about being a melanin child of God. Just like everything else in life, it goes on, and a generation change is always inevitable.

I understand this, but with that said, I just can't relate to the molly consuming rappers sporting rainbow color hair and multiple facial tattoos. Also, these street life rappers weighing a buck O-5, drinking lean, wearing skinny jeans, and sporting nose rings are comical. I may be the old man in the room, but the current trend is very confusing to me. However, I still commend these young cats for doing their thing and keeping the music alive. Everyone has their preference in music, politics, food, religion, and sex. Please bring back the baggy jeans, I'm begging for history to repeat itself. The skinny jeans and skin-tight shirts needs to meet its demise. The world is constantly changing and many lifestyles have become more acceptable, so whatever lifestyle you choose is perfectly fine. That's your business. However, it seems like there is a conspiracy to moisturize and dumb down the hip hop culture since the powers that be cannot eliminate Hip Hop. I'm a fan of meaningful, political, and socially conscious lyrics, with flow, and masculinity. Now don't get me wrong about the new generation of rappers. Their music does serve a useful purpose.

If you're in a gentlemen's club watching curvy young women shake their well sculpted posteriors on stage while your kicking back drinking your favorite alcoholic beverage, then the new generation of rap is entertaining. This is because you are not focusing on the lyrics being recited. You can't really even comprehend the unintelligible lyrics, so will be nodding your head to the music while your mental state is on the ass shaking. However, with that said, no matter what the current state hip hop is in, it shows how great the art form of hip hop really is. No matter how raunchy, or intellectually deficient the lyrics are, the music seems to always find a purpose.

Hip Hop continues to be an entertaining money-making machine with an ever so relevant presence to people not just in the U.S., but to people all over the world. Despite how much the corporate powers have completely dumbed down the greatest musical art form on the face of the planet. Rap music started off as New York party music, and evolved to chanting, to flowing with lyrical mastery, to gangsterism on the West Coast, to the Dirty South party music, and to the lyrical monsters of the

Mid-West. Rap went through a maze of a variety of beautiful creations to now mumbling. The mumble rap non-sense will hopefully be just a painful trend. Hip hop continues to have a pulse though. Hip hop is still alive!

50

EAZY-E

Birth Name – Eric Lynn Wright

Code Name/Moniker – E, or Eazy

Albums (solo) – Eazy – Duz – It, Str8 off the Streetz of Muthaphukkin Compton, 5150 Home 4 tha Sick, It's On (Dr. Dre) 187 um killa, and Impact of a Legend.

Compliation Albums – Eternal E, Featuring...Eazy-E, Tri-Pack, and Merry Muthafuckin X-Mas.

Favorite Album – Eazy-Duz-It

Top 3 Favorite Songs

1. Boyz-N-Da hood
2. Real Muthaphuckiin G's
3. We Want Eazy

Punchline Rhymes

"I'm rollin' hard, now I'm under control
Then wrapped my 6-4 around a telephone pole
I looked at my car and I said "Oh, brother."
I throw it in the gutter, and go buy another
Walkin' home, I see the G ride
Now Cat is drivin', Kilo on the side
As they busted a U, they got pulled over
An undercover cop in a dark green Nova."

Boyz-N-da hood – (Album) Eazy-Duz-It (1988).

It's been very well documented how Eazy-E's first attempt at rap was horrific. After patient coaching by Dr. Dre, Eazy-E was eventually able to learn the craft. With the passage of time, Eazy-E did a lot more than just learn the craft of rapping. He was able to become one of the true pioneers of West Coast rap. Eazy-E's high pitch voice is one of the most unique voices of hip hop today. Eazy was a business man first by launching his label, Ruthless Records. He was able to be the front member for one of the greatest rap groups of all-time, NWA.

No matter who actually wrote Eazy's lyrics, his high pitch voice and humor-based lyrics mixed with the street realities of the inner- city neighborhoods was appealing to all people whether you grew up in safe Suburban America or the impoverish slums. Eazy's geri curl, baseball cap, and dark shades further solidified his trademark appearance. Eazy's first solo studio album "Eazy Duz-It" was a nationwide hit excluding the exception of the North East Coast who wasn't quick to embrace hip hop filled with profanity. Eazy-E and N.W.A pushed forward regardless of the East Coast's approval.

Eazy-E's Ruthless Records had an all-star line up of Ice Cube, Dr. Dre, The DOC, Michelle, and Above the Law. Eazy later introduced the world to "Bone-Thugs-N-Harmony. Eazy was more concerned with being a businessman and finding new talent rather than just being a rapper. Rest in Peace Eazy. In my opinion, Eazy-E is a top fifty Lyrical Assassin.

49

LUPE FIASCO

Birth Name – Wasalu Muhammad Jaco

Code Name/Moniker – Lupe Fiasco

Albums – Lupe Fiasco's Food & Liquor, Lupe Fiasco's The Cool, Lasers, Food & Liquor II: The Great American Rap Album Pt. 1, Tetsuo & Youth, and Drogas Light.

Favorite Album – Lupe Fiasco's Food & Liquor

Top 3 Favorite Songs

1. Kick, Push
2. Daydreamin'
3. Real

Punchline Rhymes

"My man got a little older became a better a roller
Yea no helmet hell he'll end up killing himself
Is what his momma said but he was feeling himself
Got a little more swagger in his style
Met his girlfriend she was clapping in the crowd
Love is what was happening to him now
He said I would marry but I'm engaged to the aerials and varials
And I don't think this board is strong enough to carry two
She said bow I weigh a hundred and twenty pounds."

Kick, Push – (Album) Lupe Fiasco's Food & Liquor (2006).

Lupe Fiasco is a lyrically inclined fun-spirited hip hop artist hailing from Chicago. He is a cerebral emcee mainly touching on politics and social events. The first time I heard Lupe spit was on Kanye West's "Touch the Sky". Once I heard him spit his verse, I immediately knew Lupe was going to be a star. He didn't prove me wrong. His debut album "Lupe's Food & Liquor" exceeded my expectations. The album was a major success. At the time during Lupe's debut, there were a lot of new artists watering down the art form with a bunch of buffoonery. I commend Lupe for sticking to the format of real lyricism.

After Lupe's debut album, he proved he was no one album hit wonder. His song "Superstar" was one of the best songs of the year. Lupe recently decided to retire from rap in 2017, which is a shame. He is one of the few emcees who appeared on the rap scene in the 2000's and rapped like he was from the Golden Eras of the late eighties & early nineties. Hopefully Lupe's retirement from rap will only be brief, because the rap game needs him. Lupe Fiasco is a top fifty Lyrical Assassin.

48

BUSTA
RHYMES

Birth Name – Trevor George Smith Jr.

Code Name/Moniker – Busta Rhymes

Albums – The Coming, When Disaster Strikes…, E.L.E. (Extinction Level Event): The Final World Front, Anarchy, Genesis, It Ain't Safe No More…, The Big Bang, Back on My B.S., and the Year of the Dragon.

Favorite Album – The Big Bang

Top 3 Favorite Songs

1. New York Shit
2. Put Your Hands Where My Eyes Could See
3. In the Ghetto feat. Rick James

Punchline Rhymes

"Sure we be takin' them chances
While we search for the answers we be smokin' them cancer sticks
Police provokin' motherfuckers, we dancin'
And we be dodgin' them bullets they be poppin' off at us, shit
But yet we always romance the street
And fall in love with the hood 'til somebody come blast the heat
Always up to no good, so all of my fam could eat
See in the hood we hungry, hey nigga we playin' for keeps."

In the Ghetto feat. Rick James – (Album) The Big Bang
(2006).

B usta Rhymes fits the description of an ultra-amped up emcee filled with personality and flavor. Busta, once a member of the group "Leaders of the New School", became a very successful solo artist. Busta has had one of the most successful careers out of any rapper formerly of a group. Busta is a speed monster rapper filled with an enormous amount of energy. His stage presence makes him one of the best hip hop pure entertainers of all-time. Busta's style is one of a kind. He has the personality that will make any fan of music gravitate toward him.

His discography of hit songs are club bangers that will have you on the dance floor all night. The song "Ooh Ahh" was so far in left field you couldn't help but love it. Busta instilled a unique level of flavor in the song and the video. Busta Rhymes is a classic throwback emcee whose strongest attribute is to entertain his audience with his flamboyant personality. Busta Rhymes is appropriately named due to his ability to bust rhymes. Busta rhymes the ultra-magnetic entertaining emcee is also a top fifty Lyrical Assassin.

47

BIG SEAN

Birth Name – Sean Michael Leonard Anderson

Code Name/Moniker – Big Sean

Albums – Finally Famous, Hall of Fame, Dark Sky Paradise, Twenty 88 (with Jhene Aiko), I Decided, and Double or Nothing (with Metro Boomin).

Favorite Album – Dark Sky Paradise

Top 3 Favorite Albums

1. I Don't Fuck With You feat. E-40
2. All Your Fault feat. Kanye West
3. Supa Dupa

Punchline Rhymes

"Ho we done made it through hell and disaster
My crib done got bigger, my women got badder
You wonderin' how do you get in the game
I'm wonderin' how do I get to the rafters
Oh boy, I'm mad until these records gettin' shattered
Til I'm MJ or Magic, oh she just want the status, so
You the man she got, but I'm the man she been after
She done sent so many naked pics my phone ain't got no data."

All Your Fault feat. Kanye West – (Album) Dark Sky
Paradise (2015).

Big Sean is one of the new generational emcees that I happen to have much respect for their talent. Some people have it, and some people don't. Big Sean happens to have the swagger along with smooth lyrics to garner my attention and I recognize him as a legitimate emcee. Take notice, Big Sean has the ability to land some hot little mamas such as Naya Rivera, Ariana Grande, and currently the lovely Jhene Aiko. Therefore, the brother got well-rounded game, both lyrically, and romantically. Unlike the rappers of today, Big Sean spits hot lyrics with a little humor.

You can fully understand what he is rapping about and Big Sean represents the "D" from the Midwest and he has a flow similar to the great emcees from the East Coast. The song "I Don't Fuck with You" has to be the best diss song about an ex-lover ever made. The hit is my theme song every time I think about a stupid, lunatic, and ignorant ex-girlfriend. Hopefully, my man Big Sean continues to represent hip hop in the right context, before something worse than mumble rap emerges from the pits of hell. Big Sean is a top fifty Lyrical Assassin.

46

HEATHER B

Birth Name – Heather B. Gardner

Code Name/Moniker – Heather B.

Albums – Takin Mine, Eternal Affairs

Favorite Album – Takin Mine

Top 3 Favorite Songs

1. If Headz Only Knew
2. All Glocks Down
3. Takin Mine

Punchline Rhymes

"Demolition done, competition none

Reputation unsung strong long ground what
I got verbals, got herbals, and antihistamines
I'm herbally and verbally distributin you listenin
It's more to it, than a Lex and duplex
Don't sell sex or 'mote sex sells, I got more respect
Dressed in jeans, Gortex and striped rugbies
With the strength of fifty-four niggas, word, that love me."

If Headz Only Knew – (Album) Takin' Mine (1996).

H eather B is a raw and lyrically deadly female emcee, who I first heard on Boogie Down Productions "7 Dee Jays". Heather B is blessed with an authoritarian voice and an East Coast flow I adore. She appeared on the reality show "The Real World," voicing her determination to make it in the rap world. Heather B's debut album "Takin Mine" was an underrated success. I'm not sure why there was such a long delay between her only two albums. Heather B was a top-notch lyricist who could fire off hype rhymes effortlessly. It may seem ridiculous, but Heather B's mesmerizing flow is something similar to how Biggie use to flow. Therefore, it is mind boggling to me why Heather B didn't have more success in the rap game.

There is absolutely no reason why Heather B shouldn't be on everyone's list of top five female emcees. She has the voice, lyrics, flow, and raw energy on the microphone. Heather B left a lot on the table by only delivering two albums. However, I would like to commend her on her short-lived success. Heather B is a top fifty Lyrical Assassin.

45

BIG MIKE

Birth Name – Michael Barnett

Code Name/Moniker – Big Mike, The PeterMan, and Nawlins' Phats.

Albums – Somethin' Serious, Still Serious, Hard to Hit, and Nawlins' Phats.

Favorite Album – Still Serious

Top 3 Favorite Songs

1. Playa, Playa
2. Burban & Impalas
3. Playas to Governors

Punchline Rhymes

"I was a curious child
I used to hang out by the ballroom and study the gangsta style
The way they talk, the way they walk, the way they act
The way they wore that gangsta hat
Tilted, rim laid flat out
Now that's the type of shit I'm talkin about
Yeah, cigarette in one hand, drink in the other
Leanin to one side, cooler than a motherfucker."

Straight Gangsterism Geto Boys (Album) Till Death Do Us
Part (1993).

Big Mike exploded on the rap scene when Willie D left the Geto Boys and Big Mike temporarily filled the large void. Big Mike did more than fill a void, he admirably held his own in one of the top five rap groups of all-time. I hated to see my man Wille D leave at the time, but Big Mike immediately stood out with verses on "6 Feet Deep" and "Straight Gangsterism" on the Geto Boys album "Till Death Do Us Part". Big Mike left Geto Boys when Willie D returned, but the recognition he acquired with the Geto Boys led him to delivering two very successful albums.

Big Mike has a southern drawl, while spitting his entertaining lyrics. He is an above average rhymer with lyrics that would easily meet the average hip hop fan's approval. Big Mike is one of the best emcees in the dirty south and he is a top fifty Lyrical Assassin.

44

BLACK THOUGHT

Birth Name – Tariq Luqmaan Trotter

Code Name/Moniker – Black Thought

Albums (solo) – The Live Mixtape (with J. Period), Streams of Thought Vol. 1 (with 9th Wonder & The Soul Council), and The Talented Mr. Trotter.

Albums (with The Roots) – Organix, Do You Want More?!!!??!, Illadelph, Halflife, Things Fall Apart, Phrenology, The Tipping Point, Game Theory, Rising Down, How I Got Over, Undun, …And Then You Shoot Your Cousin, and End Game.

Favorite Album – Game Theory with The Roots

Top 3 Favorite Songs

1. Game Theory
2. Don't Feel Right
3. Come Together feat. Zion

Punchline Rhymes

"This is a game, I'm your specimen
You've got to let me know baby
So I can go, I'd have to fake it
I could not make it
You could not take it

Yeah, where I'ma start it at, look I'ma part of that
Downtown Philly where it's realer than a heart attack
It wasn't really that ill until the start of crack."

Game Theory – The Roots (Album) Game Theory (2006).

Black Thought is the lead lyricist of the live instrumental rap group "The Roots". The Illadelphia rapper from Philadelphia is a savvy lyrical technician. Black Thought fires off rhymes of social consciousness and about the inner city struggles of the youth. He is a highly underrated rapper who doesn't receive enough credit for his lyrical mastery. Black Thought with The Roots has been consistent in delivering entertaining albums along with fire lyrics that make you smile. He has a nice East Coast flow that always rhymes on rhythm. Black Thought could have easily been a successful solo artist, but he remained loyal to his band members. Black Thought's watery flow and sharp lyrics makes him a top forty-five Lyrical Assassin.

43

NICKI MINAJ

Birth Name – Onika Tanya Maraj

Code Name/Moniker-Nicki Minaj

Albums – Pink Friday, Pink Friday: Roman Reloaded, The Pinkprint, and Queen.

Favorite Album – Pink Friday

Top 3 Favorite Songs

1. Moment 4 Life feat. Drake
2. No Frauds feat. Drake & Lil Wayne
3. Did it On'em

Punchline Rhymes

"I fly with the stars in the skies,
I am no longer trying to survive,
I believe that life is a prize,
But to live doesn't mean you're alive,
Don't worry bout me and who I fire
I get what I desire it's my empire
And yes I call the shots I am the umpire
I sprinkle holy water upon the vampire."

Moment 4 Life – (Album) Pink Friday (2010).

Nicki Minaj, the Queen of Queens is a bad ass female emcee. Nicki is blessed with the epitome of the "It" factor. She is a gorgeous work of art, blessed with Grade A beauty and sex appeal that has captured the hearts of both men and women. This includes those who are and are not die-hard Hip Hop fans. Nicki is like an adorable life-sized Barbie Doll with a cute and quirky rap style. Nicki successfully emulated the style of female emcees from the nineties. She put her own twist on the dynamics of a female emcee that makes her the leader of the pack that can't be touched.

Since Nicki arrived on the rap scene, she hasn't looked back. She continues to deliver one hit song after another. She has remained more relevant than any female emcee in the past decade. Nicki can do a song and a video with a garbage rapper and make the song and video entertaining. She is the Alpha Goddess on the microphone, capturing your undivided attention with one hot verse after another. Nicki remains one of the hottest female emcees in the game today. Nicki is winning and striking misery at all the haters who despise her. The most bad ass female emcee in the game today, is also a top fifty Lyrical Assassin.

42

SNOOP DOGG

Birth Name – Calvin Cordozar Broadus Jr.

Code Name/Moniker – Snoop Dogg, Snoop Doggy Dogg, Bigg Snoop Dogg, Uncle Snoop, Snoop Lion, Snoopzilla, Doggfather, Snoop Rock, Niggarachi, West Fest, and DJ Snoopadellic.

Albums (solo) – Doggstyle, The Doggfather, Da Game Is to Be Sold, Not to Be Told, No Limit Top Dogg, The Last Meal, Paid tha Cost to Be da Boss, R&G (Rhythm & Gangsta): The Masterpiece, The Blue Carpet Treatment, Ego Trippin', Malic n Wonderland, Doggumentary, Reincarnated, Bush, Coolaid, Neva Left, and Bible of Love.

Collaboration Albums – Tha Eastsidaz (with Tha' Eastsidaz), Duces 'n Trayz: The Old Fashioned Way (with Tha Eastsidaz), The Hard Way, Mac & Devin Go to High School (with Wiz Khalifa), 7 Days of Funk (with 7 Days of Funk), Royal Fam (with The Broadus Boyz), and Cuzznz (with Daz Dillinger).

Favorite Album – Doggystyle

Top 3 Favorite Songs

1. Woof feat. Fiend and Mystikal
2. Gin and Juice
3. Drop Its Likes It Hot feat. Pharrell Williams

Punchline Rhymes

"Sho' 'nuff
I keep my hand on my gun, cause they got me on the run
Now I'm back in the courtroom waitin' on the outcome
Free 2Pac is all that's on a nigga's mind
But at the same time it seems, they tryin' to take mine
So I'mma get smart and get defensive and shit
And put together a Million March for some gangsta shit."

2 of Amerikaz Most Wanted 2pac feat. Snoop Dogg –
(Album) All Eyez On Me (1996).

S noop Dogg has been on the rap scene since breaking through on the "Deep Cover" Soundtrack in the early nineties with Dr. Dre. Snoop and Dre shifted the rap momentum to the West Coast that reigned supreme for many years in the nineties. Snoop's laid-back flow with Dre. Dre's genius like beats prove to be a perfect chemistry for rap royalty. Snoop's debut album "Doggystyle" was one of the most anticipated albums in hip hop history. Snoop didn't disappoint, delivering a platinum album with Dre's superior production.

It didn't matter if it was "Death Row" or "No Limit", Snoop continued to do his thing. Snoop collaborated with Pharrell Williams and delivered the party song of the year "Drop It Like It's Hot". Snoop tested the boundaries by doing a successful family show "Snoop Dogg's Father Hood". Also, he created a successful song by testing his singing skills on "Sensual Seduction". Today Snoop remains relevant in hip hop and he has established his legacy as being a certified legend. Snoop Dogg, a true West Coast legend and hip hop All-Star is also a top forty-five Lyrical Assassin.

41

FOXY BROWN

Birth Name – Inga DeCarlo Fung Marchand

Code Name/Moniker – Foxy Brown

Albums – Ill Na Na, Chyna Doll, Broken Silence, and King Soon Come.

Favorite Album – Ill Na Na

Top 3 Favorite Songs

1. Get You Home feat. Blackstreet
2. (Holy Matrimony) Letter to the Firm
3. I'll Be feat. Jay-Z

Punchline Rhymes

"Thug niggas give they minks to chinks, tore down
We sip drinks, rockin' minks, flashin' rings and things
Frontin' hardcore deep inside the Jeep, mackin'
Doin' my thing, fly nigga, you a Scarface king
Bitches grab ya ta-ta's, get them niggas for they chedda'
Fuck it, Gucci sweaters and Armani leathers
Flossin' rocks like the size of Fort Knox
Four carats, the ice rocks, pussy bangin' like Versace locs pops."

I Shot Ya (Remix) LL Cool J feat. Keith Murray, Prodigy,
Foxy Brown, & Fat Joe – (Album) Mr. Smith (1995).

F oxy Brown was the first female I can re-call with a supreme level of swagger on the microphone. Her voice, rhymes, and sex appeal were the introduction of a new female emcee breaking through in the mid-nineties.

However, Lil Kim was the first to do it. Foxy had fire lyrics she recited with bravado and she was great with rhyming on beat. Earlier in her career, Foxy was rhyming with Nas and Jay-Z, so she was getting schooled by raps heavy weights, who coached her well in emceeing.

Her contributions on the "Firm" album help make it classic material today. Foxy's rhymes on "Paper Chase" with Jay-Z got the song onto my favorite Jay-Z tracks. Foxy had many feuds with other female emcees, but Foxy was a standout female lyricist with style, lyrics, and a smooth silky flow. Foxy Brown is a top forty-five Lyrical Assassin.

40

THE GAME

Birth Name – Jayceon Terrell Taylor

Code Name/Moniker – The Game, Game

Albums – The Documentary, Doctor's Advocate, LAX, The R.E.D. Album, Jesus Piece, The Documentary 2.5, 1992, and Westside Story.

Favorite Album – The Documentary

Top 3 Favorite Songs

1. It's Okay (One Blood) feat. Junior Reid
2. Dreams
3. Hate It or Love It feat. 50 Cent

Punchline Rhymes

"I woke up out that coma 2001
'bout the same time Dre dropped 2001
Three years later the album is done
Aftermath presents: Nigga Witta Attitude, Volume One
Rap critics politickin, wanna know the outcome
Ready to Die, Reasonable Doubt and Doggystyle in one
I feel like 'Pac after the Snoop Dogg trial was done
Dre behind that G series and All Eyez on Me."

Dreams – (Album) The Documentary (2005).

The Game resurrected the West Coast after it seem like there was a dirty south takeover. The Game came out on fire show casing his skills along side 50 Cent. Two rappers with strong personalities make it hard to co-exist for any extended period of time. The Game separated himself from 50 Cent and kept moving forward delivering hot singles in the process. The Game is just not a gangster on the microphone rapping.

The Game has hard core lyrics with a sick flow. The Game strongholds the microphone with extreme confidence using his grizzle voice to inform you he is confident in what he is saying. The Game put the whole West Coast on his shoulders in the early and mid-2000's, keeping the West Coast spirit alive. His presence in hip hop opened the door for another great emcee, Kendrick Lamar. The Game saved the West Coast and I consider him to be a top forty Lyrical Assassin.

39

JERU THE DAMAJA

Birth Name – Kendrick Jeru Davis

Code Name/Moniker – Jeru the Damaja

Albums – The Sun Rises in the East, Wrath of the Math, Heroz4Hire, Divine Design, Still Rising, and The Hammer.

Favorite Album – The Sun Rises in the East

Top 3 Favorite Songs

1. Ain't the Devil Happy
2. The Frustrated N****
3. Jungle Music

Punchline Rhymes

"I hate when the devil's happy, so I wear my hair hair nappy
Knotty, won't go out like john gotti
He came from the caves to destroy everybody
And we like fools destroy our own bodies
Too many n**** chillin, bad boys boom boom

This leaves no room for the flowers to bloom
Seeds blow in the wind, another drug killing
What, are we accomplishing? Nothing."

Ain't the Devil Happy – (Album) The Sun Rises in the East
(1994).

J eru the Damaja is another one of those great New York lyricists that was heavily slept on in the 90's. I'm guilty of never purchasing a Jeru the Damaja album. After rap being extremely watered down in the 2000's, I can now appreciate a great lyricist that didn't receive nationwide fanfare. The hit song "Ain't the Devil Happy" is one of the best Hip Hop songs I didn't recognize until many years later. A brilliant song with a powerful socially conscious message. The song was a perfect examination of the ills of society in the early and mid-90's. The beat is something sent from heaven above. Jeru deserved more credit as a technically efficient emcee. Jeru the Damaja is a top forty Lyrical Assassin.

38

SPECIAL ED

Birth Name – Edward Archer

Code Name/Moniker – Special Ed

Albums – Youngest in Charge, Legal, Revelations, The Best of Special Ed, and Still Got It Made.

Favorite Album – Youngest in Charge

Top 3 Favorite Songs

1. Come On, Let's Move It
2. I Got it Made
3. I'm the Magnificent

Punchline Rhymes

"I spent time with the rhyme like a person
Rehearsin like a verse in a chapter
Of a play, but I rap to
Not make money
Though you might find it funny
But hey, I do it cause I like it, plus it is constructive
Enriching to the mind, cause it's mentally productive
And I am one who seeks special education."

                    Come On, Let's Move It – (Album) Legal (1990).

S pecial Ed was another great 80's era rapper. He was the pretty boy rapper in the late 80's and early 90's who was "that guy" laced with sharp lyrics. Special Ed sported slick sport jackets with no gold chains and he wore stylish silk shirts with matching pants. He had a smooth player vibe, similar to Big Daddy Kane, but not as flashy. Special Ed was a smooth lyricist with humorous braggadocio rhymes. Special Ed's debut album "Youngest in Charge" immediately place him in the category of one of New York's top emcees at that time. Special Ed's sophomore album "Legal" proved Special Ed was no fluke. Special Ed made significant contributions to the hip hop world with incredible hit songs. Unfortunately, by the late 90's Special Ed faded away. However, I believe Special Ed has enough impressive work to be a top forty Lyrical Assassin.

37

SPICE 1

Birth Name – Robert Lee Green Jr.

Code Name/Moniker – Spice 1, The Eastbay Gangsta

Album (solo) – Spice 1, 187 He Wrote, Amerikkka's Nightmare, 1990 – Sick, The Black Bossalini, Immortalized, The Last Dance, Spiceberg Slim, The Ridah, Dyin' 2 Ball, The Truth, Haterz Nightmare, and Throne of Game.

Collaboration Albums – Criminal Activity (with Criminalz), NTA: National Thug Association (with Bad Boy), The Pioneers (with MC Eiht), Thug Lordz Trilogy (with Thug Lordz), Keep it Gangsta (with MC Eiht), Criminal Intent (with Jayo Felony) and Thug Therapy (with Bossolo).

Punchline Rhymes

"I'm sick up in this game
I'll take no secondary shorts and
Slam dunk these riddles up in yo' chest like Jordan
Menace II Society mad man killer
Just call me the East Bay Gangsta
Neighborhood drug dealer
Quick to make decisions and I'm
Quick to get my blast on."

Trigga Gots No Heart – (Album) Menace II Society
Soundtrack (1993).

S pice 1, the Eastbay Gangsta was on fire in the early 90's when gangster rap was on the rise. Spice 1 was more than a contributor to the gangster rap genre when the West Coast executed a takeover of the rap game. Spice 1 was one of the leading field generals of West Coast rap. His witty West Coast rhymes help launch himself in the fore-front of rap's wild wild West. Spice 1 along with E-40 were the influential figures of the Bay Area rappers.

Spice 1 was the first rapper I ever heard use the stutter rap on his hit single "Money Gone". No one mastered that art form better than Spice 1. Twenty-five years later after Spice 1's debut, his songs still sound good. The OG Spice 1 is one of the top five West Coast emcees of all-time. Also, Spice 1 is a top-forty Lyrical Assassin.

36

JADAKISS

Birth Name – Jason Terrance Phillips

Code Name/Moniker – Jadakiss

Albums (solo) – Kiss the Game Goodbye, Kiss of Death, The Last Kiss, Top 5 Dead or Alive.

Collaboration Album (with The Lox) – Friday on Elm Street (with Fabolous).

Favorite Album – Kiss of Death

Top 3 Favorite Songs

1. Why feat. Anthony Hamilton
2. Checkmate
3. U Make Me Wanna feat. Mariah Carey

Punchline Rhymes

"You want to know why I invest all my money into haze and into dope
'cause right now, I'm currently a slave for Interscope
Respect first, then money- basic shit
If you got niggaz under pressure, you could take they shit
Listen, I'ma leave you right where you stand
Have the ambulance pass ya Timberlands off right to ya man
'cause he pussy, he ain't gonna do nothin but look
When it come to beef, he don't want to do nothing but cook."

Rite Where U Stand-Gang Starr (Album) The Ownerz
(2003).

J adakiss, the raspy voice lyricist was one third of the rap group, "The Lox". Jadakiss has flown under the radar as far as popularity, but in any Hip-Hop circle he is a respected emcee. Also, Jadakiss is a lyrically inclined rapper. His signature cough before and after versus is a reminder of his originality. Jadakiss is also an accomplished diss artist by Jadakiss successfully clapping back with the song "Checkmate". In the heat of a battle of a diss conflict, the more supreme lyricist usually comes out of the battle victorious.

Lyrics are the roots of superiority. Jadakiss is the definition of a New York superior lyricist. The song "Why" on the "Kiss of Death", made me seriously take notice of Jadakiss' skills. Jadakiss spit one fire verse after another on the hit song. The content on "Why" was a display of political content touching on issues of the judicial system, prison life, Hollywood, the music industry, snitching, and Presidential affairs. Jadakiss is one of the rappers who gave me inspiration to write this book. He deserves more recognition than he received. The NY flow is embedded in his soul. Jadakiss is an underrated top forty Lyrical Assassin.

35

FAT JOE

Birth Name – Joseph Antonio Cartagena

Code Name/Moniker – Fat Joe, Joey Crack

Albums – Represent, Jealous One's Envy, Don Cartagena, Jealous One's Still Envy, Loyalty, All or Nothing, Me, Myself, and I, The Elephant in the Room, Jealous One's Still Envy 2, The Darkside Vol. 1, and Family Ties.

Collaborative Albums – Plata O Plomo

Mixtapes – The Crack Era, The Darkside Vol. 2, and The Darkside Vol. 3.

Favorite Album – Jealous One's Still Envy

Top 3 Favorite Songs

1. So Much More
2. Flow Joe
3. All the Way Up feat. Remy Ma

Punchline Rhymes

"Cost you when my lid just twist to one side
We don't bitch we don't snitch we stick and just ride and I...
Never gave a fuck about po po
Niggas so gangsta make a songs about my 4 4
My my 4 4 4 4
Gets worse $$$ shit when i visit the church
I'm down with TDJanks kerk flankins
Better have my overlin plate filled with franklins blastin me."

So Much More – (Album) All or Nothing (2005).

F at Joe is another rap veteran who has been relevant in the rap game for a very long time. Fat Joe has steadily remained a force in Hip Hop by dropping hit singles on a consistent basis. Fat Joe the leader of Terror Squad has led his clique admirably through the trenches of the highly competitive Hip Hop society. Joe represents the East Coast flavor of New York street rhymes with a tough grimy style. Fat Joe doesn't get enough credit for his rhymes and flow.

Joe has been quite versatile by collaborating with some of R&B's heavy weights. My man Fat Joe has established his mark in hip hop society by generating an impressive track list of Hip Hop classics. Fat Joe is most definitely a top thirty-five Lyrical Assassin.

34

TOO SHORT

Birth Name – Todd Anthony Shaw

Code Name/Moniker – Too Short, Short Dog

Albums – Don't Stop Rappin', Players, Raw, Uncut & X-Rated, Born to Mack, Life Is…Too Short, Short Dog's in the House, Shorty the Pimp, Get in Where You Fit In, Cocktails, Gettin' It (Album Number Ten), Can't Stay Away, You Nasty, Chase the Cat, What's My Favorite Word?, Married to the Game, Blow the Whistle, Get Off the Stage, Still Blowin', No Trespassing, The Pimp Tape, The Sex Tape.

Collaboration Albums – Dangerous Crew (with The Dangerous Crew), Don't Try This at Home (with The Dangerous Crew), History: Mob Music (with E-40), History: Function Music (with E-40), Pimpin Incorporated.

Extended Play – Respect the Pimpin', 19,999: The EP

Favorite Album – Life Is…Too Short

Top 3 Favorite Songs

1. Gettin' It
2. Don't Fight the Feeling feat. Danger Zone & Rappin 4-Tay
3. Freaky Tales

Punchline Rhymes

"Everything you dreamed of, never have to front
You should be getting it, getting money
I'm talking bout you black, don't laugh it ain't funny
You should get a good lawyer, like Johnny Cochran
Swear to tell the truth, hell no I didn't pop him
Get your kids in school, so they can get an education
Get a degree, and take a vacation."

Gettin' It feat. Parliament-Funkadelic – (Album) Gettin' It
(Album Number Ten) (1996).

Pimping, pimping, and more pimping is what you think about when you hear Too Short's name. As a grown conscious deeply spiritual man, I cringe when I hear some of the lyrics of pimping. Also, I'm very disturbed with the recent travesties of sex trafficking, with young beautiful and innocent young women forced into sex. The act of pimping is sickening, disgusting, and inhumane. However, that is another topic for another time and place. Too Short explicitly talked about pimping in his songs that I shamefully admit were extremely entertaining and humorous.

If you were growing up in the eighties and nineties and love to blast your music out of the most powerful woofers money could buy, then nine times out of ten you were listening to the powerful beats of a Too Short song. Less than two years ago, I went to a Too Short concert and I couldn't believe how many gorgeous women attended the concert, both young and old. I was truly amazed at no matter how raunchy the lyrics are women of many ages love his music. Too Short had his signature chant of "Biiiiiiiiiiitch," that made him so popular. Too Short, unlike many of the great ones was able to experience longevity in the rap game.

Too Short has solidified his spot in rap greatness even without the support of the East Coast, where he was widely unpopular in the late eighties and early nineties. Too Short's rhymes put a smile on my face on many gloomy days. Too Short no doubt is a top thirty-five Lyrical Assassin.

33
PRODIGY

Birth Name – Albert Johnson

Code Name/Moniker – Prodigy

Albums (with Mobb Deep) – Juvenile Hall, The Infamous, Hell on Earth, Murda Muzik, Infamy, Amerikaz Nightmare, Blood Money, and The Infamous Mobb Deep.

Albums (solo) – H.N.I.C, H.N.I.C Pt. 2, H.N.I.C 3, The Bumpy Johnson Album, Hegelian Dialectic (The Book of Revelation).

Collaboration Albums – Return of the Mack (with the Alchemist), Product of the 80's (with Big Twins & Un Pacino), Albert Einstein (with the Alchemist), Young Rollin Stonerz (with Boogz Boogetz).

Favorite Album – Return of the Mac (with the Alchemist)

Top 3 Favorite Songs

1. Bang on 'Em
2. Stuck on You
3. Pretty Thug

Punch Line Rhymes

"There's a war goin' on outside no man is safe from
You could run but you can't hide forever
From these streets that we done took
You walkin' witcha head down scared to look
You shook 'cause ain't no such things as halfway crooks
They never around when the beef cooks in my part of town
It's similar to Vietnam
Now we all grown up and old, and beyond the cop's control."

Survival of the Fittest – (Album) The Infamous (1995).

P rodigy (may he rest in peace), is another great rapper who passed away in his forties. Prodigy was the latest to fall victim to this disturbing trend. It makes me think are these deaths accidental, coincidental, or intentional? It's hard to believe Prodigy passed away. However, Prodigy the other half of the great rap duo Mobb Deep made his mark on hip hop with a hit list of classic music. Prodigy had a laid-back flow with gritty rhymes of hood life in the NYC. Prodigy's "Return of the Mac" album with The Alchemist was an underrated classic filled with great production.

The murder raps of Prodigy signified the excellence of the album. Prodigy trademarked the term "H.N.I.C" in Hip Hop, and he made a series of albums under the empowering title. Mobb Deep will go down as one of the top ten rap duos of all time. Prodigy as a solo artist was an accomplished emcee with a street rap certified pedigree. Prodigy, may he rest in peace, is a top thirty-five Lyrical Assassin.

32

TREACH

Birth Name – Anthony Criss

Code Name/Moniker – Treach

Albums (with Naughty by Nature) – Independent Leaders, Naughty by Nature, 19 Naughty III, Poverty's Paradise, Nineteen Naughty Nine: Nature's Fury, IIcons, Anthem Inc.

Favorite Album (with Naughty by Nature) – Naughty by Nature

Top 3 Favorite Songs

1. Let the Ho's Go
2. Everything's Gonna Be Alright
3. Uptown Anthem

Punchline Rhymes

"Some get a little and some get none
Some catch a bad one and some leave the job half done
I was one who never had and always mad
Never knew my dad, mother fuck the fag
Where anyway I didn't pick up, flipped the clip up
Too many stick-ups, 'cause niggas had the trigger hic-ups
I couldn't get a job, nappy hair was not allowed
My mother couldn't afford us, she had to throw me out."

Everything's Gonna Be Alright – (Album) Naughty by
Nature (1991).

Treach was part of the trio of super rap group Naughty by Nature. Treach was a lyrical beast in his heyday with Naughty by Nature. Treach possessed a fast pace flow laced with explosive lyrics. Treach is in the category of emcees with the best flows rap has ever witnessed. His ability to compact his rhymes and recite them in a continuous format, was far more advanced than his peers in the early nineties.

Naughty by Nature was a highly entertaining rap group led by Treach's uncanny ability to galvanize his audience with his lyrical ability and catchy hooks. Treach could have easily been a successful solo artist. However, he didn't stray away from his roots of being a member of a great rap group. Treach doesn't get enough credit as a lyricist due to no activity (to my knowledge) as a solo artist. In my book, Treach is a top thirty-five Assassin.

31

KANYE WEST

Birth Name – Kanye Omari West

Code Name/Moniker – Yeezy, Ye

Albums – The College Dropout, Late Registration, Graduation, 808 & Heartbreak, My Beautiful Dark Twisted Fantasy, Watch the Throne, Yeezus, The Life of Pablo, and ye.

Favorite Album – Late Registration

Top 3 Favorite Songs

1. Heard Em Say feat. Adam Levine
2. Diamonds from Sierra Leone
3. Can't Tell Me Nothing

Punchline Rhymes

"Penitentiary chances, the devil dances
And eventually answers to the call of Autumn
All of them fallin' for the love of ballin'
Got caught with thirty rocks, the cop look like Alec Baldwin
Inter century anthems based off inner city tantrums
Based off the way we was branded
Face it, Jerome get more time than Brandon
And at the airport they check all through my bag."

Gorgeous – (Album) My Beautiful Dark Twisted Fantasy
(2010).

I thought long and hard about placing Kanye on this list. A year ago, it would have been a no brainer for me to recognize Kanye as one Hip Hop's best. It's extremely difficult for me to accept the recent ridiculous comments Kanye has made about slavery. Kanye rightfully called out Bush years ago after his administrations lame relief response to Hurricane Katrina. Kanye's support for number 45 and his public display of donning a MAGA hat is more disrespectful than hurtful to me. His attention seeking antics are childish and selfish.

Kanye, the son of a former Black Panther father used to spit socially and politically conscious rhymes. Now his far-right support is quite disturbing and if he continues he is going to lose the majority of his fan base, no matter how great his music is. Regardless of his ignorant comments, I must be honest and without bias in my assessment. Kanye is rap's second-best producer of all-time. His flow is not advanced and sometimes barely mediocre at best. But Kanye does have nice lyrics to keep you interested in his songs while you are uncontrollably nodding your head to his advanced beats.

Kanye's latest album "ye", is simply marvelous. Kanye attempted to clean up his terrible comments on his new album "ye." I will give Kanye credit for that. Also, the album "ye" is a brilliant seven track work of art. The "ye" album is so great it helped me be more forgiving towards Kanye. The realization is that Kanye is one of the few rappers today keeping good rap music alive. Not only did Kanye produce and deliver a great album in "ye", he produced another master piece in the working on Nas's album NASIR. The song "Violent Crimes" on the "ye" album is a heartfelt display of a father treasuring his baby girl from the predatorial nature of men, who desperately try to conquer every woman in their sights. Hats off to Kanye for making the track. In hindsight, Kanye has contributed a lot to the hip hop culture with an impressive collection of great albums. His masterful work as a producer/ rapper is legendary and only second to Dr. Dre. Kanye West, whether popular or not, is a top thirty-five Lyrical Assassin.

30

DR. DRE

Birth Name – Andre Romelle Young

Code Name/Moniker – Dr. Dre

Albums (solo) – The Chronic, 2001, Compton

Album (soundtrack) – The Wash

Collaboration Album (with World Class Wreckin' Cru) – World Class, Rapped in Romance

Albums (with NWA) – N.W.A and the Possee, Straight Outta Compton, 100 Miles and Runnin', Niggaz4Life

Favorite Album – Compton

Top 3 Favorite Songs

1. Dre Day feat. Snoop Dogg
2. The Next Episode feat. Snoop Dogg
3. Animals feat. Anderson Paak

Punchline Rhymes

"I just bought California
Them other states ain't far behind it either
I remember selling instrumentals off a beeper
Millionaire before the headphones or the speakers
I was getting money 'fore the internet
Still got Eminem checks I ain't opened yet
MVP shit, this is where the trophies at
D-R-E, this is where the dope is at."

Talk About It feat. King Mez & Justus (Album) Compton
(2015).

The average hip hop fan thinks of Dr. Dre as the greatest rap producer of all-time, and that he is. I will give Dr. Dre the credit he deserves as an emcee. Dr. Dre is a very decent rapper, not great, but not poor. Dr. Dre once rapped about his accomplishments in developing and bringing the hip hop world some of the most dynamic emcees. The verse Dr. Dre delivered, was an example of his own above average lyrical skills on the microphone.

Dr. Dre is another rap veteran who has been relevant in hip hop for a very long time. He has produced some of rap's greatest albums. In the process, Dr. Dre has laid down some memorable verses as either a guest or on his own albums. Dr. Dre was responsible for the rise of the West. The momentum he created in the late eighties, created a flux of West Coast all-star rappers through the nineties. Dr. Dre is a true West Coast pioneer who eventually branched out to the East Coast to produce albums for some of the most prominent emcees East of the Mississippi.

Some of the most notable rappers in the game will call the Doctor for a fix of some dope production. Dr. Dre has done more than hold his own on the microphone. Dre is the super producer who is an accomplished emcee. The greatest producer in the history of rap music is also a top-thirty Lyrical Assassin.

29

KENDRICK LAMAR

Birth Name – Kendrick Lamar Duckworth

Code Name/Moniker – Kendrick Lamar, K-Dot

Albums – Section.80, Good Kid, M.A.A.D City, To Pimp a Butterfly, Damn

Favorite 3 Songs

1. Look Out for Detox
2. Loyalty feat. Rihanna
3. Money Trees feat. Jay Rock

Punchline Rhymes

"A demon come near and I might throw a spear at the omen
You looking at the 2010 Romans
Empire, Hiipower HP, in ya face like HD
And I spit like a HK
I'mma shot like a H3, H-U-B-C-I-T-Y, A-B and Y-G
Problem and Hootie N****
Tell the government come shoot me, n****
Cause I'm going out with a fist raised."

Look Out for Detox (2010).

K endrick Lamar represents the post Y2K generation of rappers whose lyrical skills are much more advanced than his peers. Kendrick recites his rhymes like he is literally on fire. There is no mumble in Kendrick's articulate vocabulary display of clear and concise lyrics. Hailing from Compton, Kendrick doesn't rap like the typical Compton rappers of the past. Kendrick is a lyrical beast with an array of party rhymes, with social and political awareness.

I witnessed Kendrick Lamar open up for Drake and at that very moment I knew Kendrick was going to be a force to reckon with. His act was filled with lyrics blazing like a sniper. I couldn't wait for his album "Good Kid, M.A.A.D City" to drop. The album took a little time to grow on me. However, the album solidified Kendrick's position as one of the new faces in the rap game. Present day Kendrick Lamar is on top of the Hip Hop World. I hope he continues to do what he is doing and put these mumble rappers out of business.

Kendrick Lamar has established his mark as one of the top emcees in Hip Hop today. Also, Kendrick is a top-thirty Lyrical Assassin.

28

CHUBB ROCK

Birth Name – Richard Simpson

Code Name/Moniker – Chubb Rock, The Chubbster

Albums – Chubb Rock feat. Howie Tee, And the Winner is…(with Howie Tee), The One, I Gotta Get Mine Yo, The Mind, Bridging the Gap (with Wordsmith)

Favorite Album – I Gotta Get Mine Yo

Favorite 3 Songs

1. The Hatred
2. Treat 'Em Right
3. Lost in the Storm

Punchline Rhymes

"Extremities excites pulses and in turn different entities
Won't break bread of split the peas
But in the soup the mixture of several racial groups
Minority troops flavors the broth of Wall Street suits
Armani or maybe Versace
Monetary gain can't stop me White House frolics
Judicial alcoholics
Cover up versions of death in the Persian."

The Hatred – (Album) I Gotta Get Mine Yo (1992).

C hubb Rock is one of the most underrated rappers in the history of rap music. The Chubbster didn't necessarily start off with a major spark. However, after several albums from his first album, he became a major force in the rap game with his album "The One". Chubb Rock rhymed like an intelligent student because he was a scholar. Chubb Rock attended the Ivy League School Brown University as a pre-med student. Chubb Rock started off in the late eighties hailing from Brooklyn, New York.

Therefore, he was influenced by some of rap's best emcees. The influence appeared in Chubb Rock's rhyme and flow. Chubb Rock could rock the microphone. He had a strong authoritarian, dramatic baritone voice. Chubb can deliver a political conscious song like "The Hatred" and then he can deliver a club banger like "Treat Em Right". It seems like whenever there is any type of "greatest rapper" listing Chubb Rock is missing from the list.

The lack of love for Chubb is quite disturbing to me. My man Chubb Rock is an underrated top-thirty Lyrical Assassin.

27

ROYCE DA 5'9"

Birth Name – Ryan Daniel Montgomery

Code Name/Moniker – Royce da 5'9", Nickel Nine

Albums (solo) – Rock City, Death is Certain, Independent's Day, Street Hop, Success is Certain, Layers, Book of Ryan.

Collaborative Albums – Slaughterhouse (with Slaughterhouse), Hell: The Sequel (with Bad Meets Evil), Welcome to: Our House (with Slaughterhouse), Shady XV (with Shady Records), PRhyme (with DJ Premier as PRhyme), PRhyme 2 (with DJ Premier as PRhyme).

Favorite Album – Death is Certain

Favorite 3 Songs

1. Hip Hop
2. Regardless
3. Beef

Punchline Rhymes

"Yeah, yeah, we started from nothing a couple MC's
Beat-boxin, the crowd in the lunch room (yeah)
Me and Prem', both names go together
Like they ain't supposed to be separate, like "D" in the D
I said it before, I rep in records beats
At the headquarters, rest in peace
Nigga I'ma hold shotty, and knock you out
And I ain't gotta know Karate like Afu-ra."

Hip Hop – (Album) Death is Certain (2004).

R oyce da 5'9" is a lyrically inclined emcee from Detroit, Michigan who rapped with Eminem before Em's rise to fame. To this very day Royce and Eminem are still friends and rapping together. Royce teamed with thee DJ Premier and found his path to solo fame and recognition he rightfully deserves. Royce is a legitimate rhyme sayer with an arsenal of savvy rhymes and a skillful flow. Royce has rhymed with some of the best emcees in the game by being one third of the rap group Slaughterhouse.

Royce is more than capable of carrying his own weight on the microphone. Any Hip Hop fan will agree with me, Royce da 5'9" is an efficient rhyme technician with an above average flow. Every rapper's voice is not made for DJ Premier's untouchable beats. However, Royce's delivery and rhymes are a perfect match for Premos production. A Mid-West veteran who represents Detroit as one of the Mid-West's finest. I believe Royce da 5'9" is a top-thirty Lyrical Assassin.

26

HEAVY D

Birth Name – Dwight Errington Myers

Code Name/Moniker – Heavy D, The Overweight Lover

Albums (with the Boyz) – Living Large, Big Tyme, Peaceful Journey, Blue Funk, Nuttin' But Love.

Albums (solo) – Waterbed Hev, Heavy, Vibes, Love Opus

Favorite Album – Blue Funk

Favorite 3 Songs

1. Somebody for Me
2. Who's The Man?
3. Big Daddy

Punchline Rhymes

"Yes, too many brothers be fakin' moves, or frontin' grooves
Peace to all the brothers on the block, drinkin' and passin' brew
Money tried to flip but he got flopped
Said it was his corner let him know his corner's on my block
I know your fantasy, don't Stay, I ain't Jodeci
When I used to juggle y'all was crumbs who didn't notice me
But now you see me in a magazine, on your TV screen
On the radio liver stereo lookin' clean." Who's the Man (Album) Blue
Funk (1992).

H eavy D, may he rest in peace. The Over Weight Lover was rap's greatest R&B rapper. Heavy D used sex appeal to capture his fan base with the ladies similar but different from LL Cool J. Heavy D made all the heavy-set men believe if their clothes and game were intact, they would be relevant to the finest of ladies. Jamaican born, Heavy D was not only a R&B rapper he often fused reggae vibes into his music.

He delivered his rhymes perfectly on beat using unique chants and grunts that no one else could duplicate. Heavy D was no gimmick. He was a bona-fide lyricist groomed through the golden years of rap in the late eighties. Heavy was able to out last some of the more prolific rappers in his era, sticking to the formula with a steadiness and consistent flow.

Heavy D was also a good entertainer, he had very well-choreographed dance moves while he recited his rhymes with the confidence of a suave big man. Once again, my man Heavy D may he rest in peace. Heavy D is a top-thirty Lyrical Assassin.

25

J. COLE

Birth Name – Jermaine Lamarr Cole

Code Name/Moniker – J. Cole, Therapist

Albums – Cole World: The Sideline Story, Born Sinner, 2014 Forest Hills Drive, 4 Your Eyez Only, KOD.

Compliation Album (with Dreamville) – Revenge of the Dreamers II

Favorite Album – KOD

Favorite 3 Songs

1. Motiv8
2. Neighbors
3. ATM

Punchline Rhymes

"I pay taxes, so much taxes, shit don't make sense
Where do my dollars go? You see lately, I ain't been convinced
I guess they say my dollars supposed to build roads and schools
But my niggas barely graduate, they ain't got the tools
Maybe 'cause the tax dollars that I make sure I send
Get spent hirin' some teachers that don't look like them
And the curriculum be tricking them, them dollars I spend
Got us learning about the heroes with the whitest of skin."

Brackets – (Album) KOD (2018).

J. Cole is a millennial rapper who recently has overly impressed me. His latest album "KOD", is the best rap album from start to finish that I've heard in the past ten years! J. Cole is the real deal. It is absolutely obvious he has been influenced by some of the greatest emcees who ever blessed the microphone. J. Cole represents an artist with the political and social consciousness that will always be a characteristic of greatness in my list of favorites.

J. Cole is a very skillful wordsmith who delivers one punchline after another. His recent ascension in the Hip Hop World has convinced me to believe his is on his was way to rap royalty. The dude is on fire right now and he is killing the rap game. On the song "Brackets" on "KOD", J. Cole is brilliantly going in on the intricacies of the system. On the song "1985 (Intro to "The Fall Off")" he goes in on the current rappers and the state of hip hop, similar to what I did in the preface.

J. Cole masterfully articulates himself by firing a series of top-notch rhymes. I really believe if J. Cole stays focused and continues to do what he is doing, he will not only save and keep Hip Hop alive, he is going to be the king of rap. In my opinion, J. Cole is a top twenty-five Lyrical Assassin that is ascending to be rated higher in years to come.

24

DMX

Birth Name – Earl Simmons

Code Name/Moniker – DMX, Dark Man X

Albums – It's Dark and Hell is Hot, Flesh of My Flesh, Blood of My Blood, ...And Then There was X, The Great Depression, Grand Champ, Year of the Dog...Again, Undisputed.

Favorite Album – It's Dark and Hell is Hot

Top 3 Favorite Songs

1. Intro – It's Dark and Hell is Hot
2. Get at Me Dog
3. Where the Hood At?

Punchline Rhymes

"Arf, arf.
This is a beat that I can freak to
just drop the reals.
Plus a nigga wit' the ill.
Ya'll niggas know my skills.
Ass from the grills get em' up,
split em' up, wet em' up.
And watch em' come get em' up."

Money, Power, Respect – (Album) The Lox – Money, Power,
Respect (1998).

Dark Man X is a highly aggressive rapper blessed with a strong, gruff voice. DMX represents the hardcore nation of the alpha male masculine rappers. The sight of DMX makes you think about a pit bull ready to attack the microphone with a vicious growl. Dark Man X is a hyper active growling lyrical monster. DMX's debut hit single and video "Get at Me Dog" made me take notice when I was literally half sleep. His voice awakened me and by the time the video was over I was fully wakened and amazed at what I just witnessed.

When the album dropped "Its Dark and Hell is Hot", I immediately purchased it without the slightest hesitation. I was more than satisfied with the album. I knew DMX was the new kid representing New York. After the success of two albums released in the same year, DMX had an epic performance in the hood thriller movie "Belly". DMX started his career off with more than a spark. He ran out of the starting blocks blazing like a Class A fire combusting through all inferior objects. DMX possesses one of the strongest and grueling voices in Hip Hop. Also, Dark Man X is a top twenty-five Lyrical Assassin.

23

E-40

Birth Name – Earl Stevens

Code Name/Moniker – E-40, 40 Water

Albums (solo)- Federal, In a Major Way, The Hall of Game, The Element of Surprise, Charlie Hustle: The Blueprint of a Self-Made Millionaire, Loyalty & Betrayal, Grit & Grind, Breakin'News, My Ghetto Report Card, The Ball Street Journal, Revenue Retrievin' Day Shift, Revenue Retrievin' Night Shift, Revenue Retrievin': Overtime Shift, Revenue Retrievin' Graveyard Shift, The Block Brochure: Welcome to the Soil 1, The Block Brochure: Welcome to the Soil 2, The Block Brochure: Welcome to the Soil 3, The Block Brochure Welcome to the Soil 4, The Block Brochure to the Soil 5, The Block Brochure to the Soil 6, Sharp on All 4 Corners: Corner 1, Sharp On All 4 Corners: Corner 2, The D-Boy Diary: Book 1, The D-Boy Diary: Book 2, The Gift of Gab.

Collaboration Albums – Down and Dirty (with The Click), Game Related (with The Click), Money & Muscle (with The Click), History: Function Music (with Too Short), History: Mob Music (with Too Short), Connected and Respected (with B-Legit).

Favorite Album – In a Major Way

Top 3 Favorite Songs

1. Zoom
2. Flashin
3. Choices (Yup)

Punchline Rhymes

"I never had, lobster in my life (or what?)

Or teriyaki steaks, just sardines and spam and cornflakes
Pacific Bell done put me on restriction once again
I can't call out, but you can call in
Can barely think straight, barely keep focus
My crackhead cousin spent the night (what we got) now we got roaches
(Damn!) Here lies my property, no composure
Six months behind on my mortgage, house under foreclosure."

Zoom – (Album) The Element of Surprise (1998).

E-40 is a master of inventing his own lingo. 40 Water has some of the slickest and creative names for his albums. Names like "The Hall of Game", "Charlie Hustle", "Revenue Retrievin", "My Ghetto Report Card", and "The Ball Street Journal." The names of his albums alone are a perfect personification of E-40's personality and demeanor. E-40 arrived on the scene in the early nineties when the West Coast rose up and started to dominate the rap scene.

E-40's slang was so influential he would come up with a name of a song, and the words of the song would be incorporated into every day street talk. A song like "Captain Save a Hoe", would be in your mind anytime you had a knowledge of a dude who lavishly spends money on a woman to be in a relationship or have intimate relations with her. E-40 is a West Coast veteran whose career has been long and fruitful. His up-tempo quick twitch rhyme style in the nineties was fresh and entertaining.

40 has changed up his style over the years to adapt to the current state of hip hop and like all the greats, he successfully has remained relevant for a very long time. E-40 has always been one of my favorite West Coast artists. E-40 is definitely an undisputable top twenty-five Lyrical Assassin.

22

BIG PUNISHER

Birth Name – Christopher Lee Rios

Code Name/Moniker – Big Pun, Big Punisher, Pun

Albums (solo) – Capital Punishment, Yeeeah Baby

Collaboration Album – The Album (with Terror Squad)

Favorite Album – Capital Punishment

Top 3 Favorite Songs

1. Still Not a Player feat. Joe
2. It's So Hard feat. Donnell Jones
3. Beware

Punchline Rhymes

"Yo what you thought punk, shit was sweet, now you can't sleep
Gotta keep ya eyes open wide and hide ya face from the streets
I'm like the beast with a warrant, far from alarmin'
Gave you fair warnin' now you on the stairs swallin'
I'm callin' out any rapper that I doubt, smack 'em in the mouth
Throw 'em in the yoke, BOOM!, then I knock 'em out
No doubt, Freddie Foxxx files 20-shot auto glock, blaow!
Benny blind Puerto Rock style."

Beware – (Album) Capital Punishment (1998).

Big Pun, may he rest in peace, left us far too early. Even earlier than Biggie. Pun was just getting started. Big Pun should have been on the rap scene way before he debuted. There were only a few speed rappers who were successful and Big Pun was one of them. Big Pun has one of the best flows in the history of rap. Check his incredible mind-boggling flow on the song "Twinz" with Fat Joe. I personally never heard a verse rhymed so incredibly. Big Pun was only alive to experience the success on one of his two albums he released.

The two albums leave you desiring for so much more from Pun. Unfortunately, Pun passed away before he was able to reach his prime. Big Pun's debut album "Capital Punishment" was slept on by many including myself. The album was filled with underrated classic songs packed with high pedigree rhymes. I wish Big Pun would have had the longevity of his counterpart, Fat Joe. However, Pun was able to give the hip hop world a glimpse of greatness. Big Punisher's brief contribution to the rap game makes him a top-twenty-five Lyrical Assassin.

21

TWISTA

Birth Name – Carl Terrell Mitchell

Code Name/Moniker – Twista, Tung Twista

Albums – Runnin' Off at da Mouth, Resurrection, Adrenaline Rush, Kamikaze, The Day After, Adrenaline Rush 2007, Category F5, The Perfect Storm, Dark Horse.

Favorite Album – Kamikaze

Top 3 Favorite Songs

1. One Last Time
2. Kill Us All

3. American Gangsta

Punchline Rhymes

"Standing in the midst of a hundred thousand haters
Dynamite and see-4 strapped around the waist bloody tears in my eyes
Hit the switch making sure any motherfucker in the vicinity blow away
and die
Kill'em off with an explosion get up bitches
Kamikaze on you hoes I'm the sacrificial lamb
Feelin the fury flow out of every follicle in my body."

Kill Us All – (Album) Kamizake (2004).

S peed, speed, and more speed. The Tung Twista burst on the scene in 1992 holding the title of the fastest rapper in the world according to the Guinness World Records. He was able to pronounce 598 syllables in 55 seconds. At the time, I was thinking Tung Twista was just a gimmick. There were periods of inactivity or not enough national exposure for Twista. Twista re-surfaced nationally on Do or Die's "Po Pimp".

The hit single re-introduced the rap community to Twista who by then dropped the "Tung" from his rap name. Twista followed up with the hit album "Adrenaline Rush." After the success of "Adrenaline Rush", Twista teamed up with the Speednot Mobtaz, but seemed to go back to a semi-hibernation period. Twista is a perfect example of resilience. He continued to grind hard and he perfected his craft while he mastered the speed flow. Twista spits fire lyrics like an inferno ripping through a forest destroying everything in sight. The emergence of Kanye West was perfect timing for Twista. Twista dropped "Kamikaze" and he murdered the rap game in 2004.

Twista finally got the well-deserved exposure that was long over-due. Twista didn't stop after his new found national success. Twista delivered a string of high quality albums and mixtapes. There are a few rappers who are on Twista's level with the speed flow. However, Twista is the greatest of them all. A lyrical gymnast with an amazing uncanny ability to recite words with the speed of lightning. Twista is a top twenty-five Lyrical Assassin.

20

SLICK RICK

Birth Name – Richard Martin Lloyd Walters

Code Name/Moniker – Slick Rick, Rick the Ruler, MC Ricky D

Albums – The Great Adventures of Slick Rick, The Ruler's Back, Behind Bars, The Art of Storytelling.

Favorite Album – The Great Adventures of Slick Rick

Top 3 Favorite Songs

1. Children's Story
2. Hey Young World
3. Mona Lisa

Punchline Rhymes

"Once upon a time not long ago
When people wore pajamas and lived life slow
When laws were stern and justice stood
And people were behavin' like they ought ta good
There lived a lil' boy who was misled
By anotha lil' boy and this is what he said
"Me, Ya, Ty, we gonna make sum cash
Robbin' old folks and makin' tha dash."

                    Children's Story (Album) The Great Adventures of Slick Rick
                                                                    (1988).

S lick Rick is rightfully dubbed as the greatest rap story teller of all time. Slick started off as a side kick to Doug E. Fresh. Doug and Slick collaborated on "The Show" and "Ladi Dadi" as I mentioned in the preface. Slick Rick was outshining Doug on those classic tracks. Slick Rick instantly stands out on a track with his British accent (he was born in London) and his flawless flow. Slick Rick will put your mind in a world of imagination and tell you a story that makes you feel like you are there witnessing the events taking place in the song.

His knack of illustrating amazing story-telling ability is MC Ricky D's signature trademark in the genre of hip hop. Slick's debut album "The Great Adventures of Slick Rick" was filled with entertaining stories of adolescence, love, child delinquency, STD's, male and female relationships, and just plain bad luck. MC Ricky D was able to put a positive message in many of his story-telling tales. Slick Rick was on fire after his debut album dropped. However, Slick Rick had an issue with a family member that led him to shooting him.

The act landed Slick Rick in prison and it interfered with his momentum. Without the prison stint, Slick would have delivered more top-notch albums like his first album. On the strength of "The Great Adventures of Slick Rick" Slick Rick had already established his mark in the rap game. A unique voice, slick rhymes, and a watery flow, Slick Rick is a top-twenty Lyrical Assassin.

19

QUEEN LATIFAH

Birth Name – Dana Elaine Owens

Code Name/Moniker – Queen Latifah

Albums – All Hail the Queen, Nature of a Sista, Black Reign, Order in the Court, The Dana Owens Album, Trav'lin' Light, Persona.

Favorite Album – Order in the Court

Top 3 Favorite Songs

1. Jersey
2. Brownsville feat. Le Fem Markita & Nikki D
3. Black hand Side

Punchline Rhymes

"When I think of home I think of a place where there's love over-flowin'
And all my family and peeps I knew when I was growin
Mommy and daddy made me proud to an Owens
Taught me to keep goin'
Straight up but never knowin'
I would become Her eminence and royal highness
The Queen Latifah; no doubt; one of New Jersey's finest
So, set if off."

Jersey – (Album)-New Jersey Drive Soundtrack (1995).

S alt-N-Pepa were the first females in rap to reach super stardom. MC Lyte was the first solo female rap artist to reach that same level of success. Right after MC Lyte, Queen Latifah found the throne. The New Jersey born emcee followed up after Lyte and made hip hop fans realize they really have to take females seriously in the rap game. Latifah's debut album "All Hail the Queen" included the hit song "Ladies First" feat. Monie Love. I first witnessed Queen Latifah freestyle on the hit show Rap City and I immediately knew she belonged, she blew me away.

Queen put New Jersey on the map. She became the leader of Jersey rappers who followed behind her after her success in the rap world. She influenced Naughty by Nature, Lords of the Underground, and Apache to make their mark in the hip hop nation. Queen is a very multi-talented individual. She found success in acting and television. Queen rightfully was awarded with a variety of acting and feminist awards. Hats off to the Queen whose fierce lyrics and East Coast flow brought a smile to my face. She is the Queen royalty of Hip Hop, and Latifah is a top-twenty Lyrical Assassin.

18

GURU

Birth Name – Keith Edward Elam

Code Name/Moniker – Guru, Gifted Unlimited Rhymes Universal, Baldhead Slick

Albums (solo)- Guru's Jazzmatazz Vol. 1, Guru's Jazmatazz Vol. 2: The New Reality, Guru's Jazzmatazz Vol. 3: Streetsoul, Baldhead Slick & da Click, Version 7.0: The Street Scriptures, Guru's Jazzmatazz, Vol. 4: The Hip Hop Jazz Messenger: Back to the Future, Guru 8.0: Lost and Found.

Albums (with Gang Starr) – No More Mr. Nice Guy, Step in the Arena, Daily Operation, Hard to Earn, Moment of Truth, The Owenerz

Favorite Album (with Gang Starr) – Hard to Earn

Top 3 Favorite Songs

1. Rite where u Stand feat. Jadakiss (with Gang Starr)
2. Code of the Streets (with Gang Starr)
3. Tonz of Gunz (with Gang Starr)

Punchline Rhymes

"Gangstarr boy and that's beyond your comprehension
Mad brothers in every city you can feel the tension
To stop the killing wack mc's must die
Who am? I'm the substance that'll make your third eye cry
Too potent, too high in intelligence quotient
when I unleash my speech I'll have you punk rappers open
I won't expose your names and your identities
You know you're phony get the fuck from in front of me."

Suckas Need Bodyguards – (Album) Hard to Earn (1994).

G uru, may the great rest in peace, is more famously the emcee of the elite group Gang Starr, including the best hip hop disc jockey of all-time DJ Premiere. Guru may have had a dry uninspiring voice, but he was strapped with a lethal arsenal of lyrics blazing. His unique voice was dominated by his skillful dosage of pure lyricism. Guru represents the Golden Era of New York hip hop even though he was from Boston, Massachusetts and Deejay Premiere was from Houston, Texas. Also, I believe Deejay Premiere was the third best rap producer of all-time.

The chemistry between Guru and Premo was beyond magical. Their sound was like no other in the game. When you listened to a Gang Starr track you would hear lyrics and beats like no other. The uniqueness of the sound was purely mesmerizing. Guru and Premo would often display their love of Jazz music and fused it into hip hop. The fusion of hip hop and jazz was the signature trademark of Gang Starr. Guru's voice was perfect for the sophisticated variety of instruments, polyrhythms, and syncopation that defines the jazz sound. Guru was a very gifted emcee and once again may he rest in peace. He is also a top-twenty Lyrical Assassin.

17

EMINEM

Birth Name – Marshall Bruce Mathers

Code Name/Moniker – Double M, M&M

Albums – Infinite, The Slim Shady LP, The Marshall Mathers LP, The Eminem Show, Encore, Relapse, Recovery, The Marshall Mathers LP 2, Revival.

Favorite Album – The Eminem Show

Top 3 Favorite Songs

1. Cleanin' Out My Closet
2. Guilty Conscience feat. Dr. Dre
3. Without Me

Punchline Rhymes

"Since I'm in a position to talk to these kids and they listen
I ain't no politician but I'll kick it with 'em a minute
Cause see they call me a menace; and if the shoe fits I'll wear it
But if it don't, then y'all'll swallow the truth grin and bear it
Now who's these king of these rude ludicrous lucrative lyrics
Who could inherit the title, put the youth in hysterics

Usin' his music to steer it, sharin his views and his merits
But there's a huge interference- they're sayin you shouldn't hear it."

Renegade feat. Eminem (Album) Jay-Z Blueprint (2001).

Eminem is the prime example of fate. The story has been well documented about how Eminem was on the verge of giving up rap music before he decided to give it on more chance. The second wind Eminem caught when his spirit was down should serve as an example for anyone who is on the verge of giving up on their dream. Fate put Eminem in the perfect place for meeting Dr. Dre whose career was in shambles after leaving Death Row. The two made magic together for many years to come. For Eminem there was a proverbial light at the end of the tunnel.

Eminem was never the person who was afraid of saying something controversial. This combined with having Dr. Dre produce the beats of his songs blew Em up like an atomic explosion. It wasn't long before Eminem had every Caucasian kid in America emulating his style, flow, and rhetoric. Eminem has a long catalog of great songs that proved he was the real deal and no phony. The movie "8 Mile" and hit song "Lose Yourself", were well received in the hip hop community. Eminem representing Detroit was very critical in the mainstream success of the other Detroit artists.

Eminem proved to the hip hop world he was no imposter or culture vulture to rap music. Soon nationwide the rap world embraced Eminem nationwide as a legitimate lyricist. In my opinion, Eminem is a top-twenty Lyrical Assassin.

16

MC LYTE

Birth Name – Lana Michelle Moorer

Code Name/Moniker – MC Lyte

Albums – Lyte as a Rock, Eyes on This, Act Like You Know, Ain't No Other, Bad As I Wanna B, Seven & Seven, Da Underground Heat Vol. 1, Legend

Favorite Album – Eyes on This

Top 3 Favorite Songs

1. Cha, Cha, Cha
2. Paper Thin
3. Poor Georgie

Punchline Rhymes

"Why, oh why did I need cappucino?
But then I calmed down, I spotted some friends
That I knew in a past life, way back when
A couple had died in a drug world
And this one guy died fightin over his girl
Another died drivin while intoxicated
Why do people make livin so complicated?"

Cappucino – (Album) Eyes on This (1989).

MC Lyte paved the way for all of the solo female rap artists in the rap game today. Salt N Pepa was a duo ruling the female class first, but MC Lyte was holding down by herself. She wasn't just using her beauty to reach stardom. Lyte was using rhyme skills and her New York flow to capture the hearts of adolescent boys like myself at the time. Her attractive girl next door looks will immediately garner your attention, while observing her album covers or staring at her while lustfully watching her on videos.

She made a teenager like myself at the time, fantasize about impregnating her after kicking some fly rhymes to me. Once Lyte pretty face forced you to listen to her, her unique sexy nasal congested voice would put you in a frenzy. If you haven't figured out by now, me having a crush on Lyte would be an understatement. She was my first celebrity heartthrob. I wanted to wife her up and spread my seeds well into the deepest depth of her ocean.

Let me get back to the subject at hand. MC Lyte was there in the thick of things in the late eighties with all of the greats of the golden years. Her debut album "Lyte As a Rock", was the defining moment that female artists were not to be slept on and placed in a box with sidekicks, video dancers, and hip-hop groupies. Lyte proved she wasn't a fluke on her sophomore album "Eyes on This." She delivered multiple hit singles on the album songs like "Cha, Cha, Cha" and "Slave 2 the Rhythm", an attack on rapper Antoinette (another gorgeous female MC) who thought it was wise to challenge the Queen of Hip Hop. MC Lyte has had a long prosperous career on the microphone. Now you can see her acting in a variety of different shows looking even better. Her melanin has treated her kindly over the years. Besides my obvious physical infatuation with the Queen of Rap, she is no joke on the microphone. MC Lyte is a top twenty Lyrical Assassin.

15

LL COOL J

Birth Name – James Todd Smith

Code Name/Moniker – Ladies Love Cool James, Uncle L

Albums – Radio, Bigger and Deffer, Walking with a Panther, Mama Said Knock You Out, 14 Shots to the Dome, Mr. Smith, Phenomenom, G.O.A.T, 10, The DEFinition, Todd Smith, Exit 13.

Favorite Album – Walking with a Panther

Top 3 Favorite Songs

1. Mama Said Knock You Out
2. Doin it
3. Back Seat

Punchline Rhymes

What the fuck? I thought I conquered the whole world
Crushed Moe Dee, Hammer, and Ice-T's girl
But still, niggaz want to instigate shit
I'll battle any nigga in tha rap game quick
Name the spot, I make it hot for ya bitches
Female rappers too, I don't give a fuck boo
Word, I'm here to crush all my peers
Rhymes of the month in The Source for twenty years."

I Shot Ya (remix) feat. Fat Joe, Foxy Brown, Prodigy, and
Keith Murray – Mr. Smith (1995).

Ladies Love Cool James was the biggest solo rap superstar in the late eighties hands down. LL was the first national lady's man on the microphone. He didn't start off that way. LL started off rocking the mic. Some people have it and some people don't. LL Cool J had the attributes when it came to sex appeal with the ladies. LL started his career off with a bold brazen in your face macho rap style.

Uncle L used his chiseled physique to appeal to women and the formula was so effective it enabled LL Cool J to remain relevant in the rap game after more advanced lyricists were able to prosper. LL Cool J is the definition of rap longevity. He left many of his peers in the eighties and early nineties by the way side, while he continued to churn out hit songs well into the 2000's. In the eighties, many rappers were using the moniker cool in some form or fashion. After seeing the video "I'm that Type of Guy", I was convinced LL was the coolest of them all. LL Cool J was a very versatile rapper. He was able to mingle with some of the young lyrical lyricists in the nineties.

The song "I Shot Ya" featuring Keith Murray, Fat Joe, Foxy Brown, and the late Prodigy was one of the best hip-hop collaborations of all-time. LL was on fire spitting hard core rhymes on the collaboration. A few years later LL appeared on the song "All I Have" and video with Jennifer Lopez displaying intense chemistry. He followed it up with having J. Lo appear on his song "Control Myself" showing the chemistry was no fluke. No one could have pulled it off twice other than LL Cool J. The day the rap Hall of Fame is built, LL deserves to have the building named after him. LL Cool J is a rap icon and a top fifteen Lyrical Assassin.

14

CAM'RON

Birth Name – Cameron Ezike Giles

Code Name/Moniker – Cam'ron, Killa Cam

Albums – Confessions of Fire, S.D.E., Come Home with Me, Purple Haze, Killa Season, Crime Pays, Heat in Here Vol. 1 (with Vado), Gunz n' Butta (with Vado), Killa Pink, The Program.

Favorite Album – Purple Haze

Top 3 Favorite Songs

1. Down and Out feat. Kanye West & Syleena Johnson
2. What Means the World
3. Get it in Ohio

Punchline Rhymes

"When I was ten got the truly dict, my uncle pulled me to the side
And he schooled me quick, told me son gooey spit
You can't get paid in a earth this big, you worthless kid
Niggas don't deserve to live, go and get a motherfucker
If he murder kids, bottle up carbohydrates and preservatives
He got hit up that same night
Ever since my flow, my dough, and my hoe game been tight."

                    Losin Weight feat. Prodigy (Album) S.D.E (2000).

S upreme swagger, swagger, and more swagger. Cam'ron is the epitome of swagger in the rap world. In the early to mid-2000's, Killa Cam was on fire delivering a string of entertaining top-flight albums. Killa Cam's swagger on the mic and off the mic is impeccable. Cam'ron delivered an epic performance as Rico in the movie "Paid in Full", portraying a New York drug dealer based on a true story. Cam made pink fashionable for macho men to sport and displaying extreme confidence while doing so. Also, Cam once owned a Pink Cadillac Escalade, it doesn't get any cockier than that.

Cam'ron has been labeled with the stigma of making up words to rhyme. Also, I've heard a critic say Cam was just flat out illiterate. It does not matter, Killa Cam has a confident lazy flow with smooth boss player like lyrics. Cam'ron is an atomic mixture of confidence and cockiness. He verbally attacked numerous rap heavy weights in the rap world with the confident demeanor of person who is very sure of himself.

Cam is a multi-talented rapper, basketball player, Harlem Hustler, and actor. The sophomore album "S.D.E" which means Sports, Drugs, Entertainment was Killa Cam's introduction to the beginning stages of rap stardom. The Song "Sports, Drugs, Entertainment" was an entertaining depiction of how Killa Cam went from being a stand out high school basketball player to having to settle for playing college ball at a Juco, to flunking out and being a full-time drug hustler. Cam's slow pace flow is mesmerizing while he expresses street tales of drug hustling.

I know many people will disagree with me, but I truly believe Cam'ron belongs in the upper echelon of elite rappers. Therefore, in my opinion Cam'ron is a top fifteen Lyrical Assassin.

13

RAEKWON

Birth Name – Corey Woods

Code Name/Moniker – Raekwon, da Chef

Albums (solo) – Only Built 4 Cuban Linx…, Immobilarity, The Lex Diamond Story, Only Built 4 Cuban Linx…Pt. II, Shaolin vs. Wu-Tang, Fly International Luxurious Art, and The Wild.

Collaboration Album – Wu-Massacre (with Method Man & Ghostface Killah).

Favorite Album – Shaolin vs. Wu-Tang

Top 3 Favorite Songs

1. Rich & Black feat. Nas
2. Rock 'N Roll feat. Ghostface Killah, Jim Jones, & Kobe
3. Catalina feat. Lfye Jennings

Punchline Rhymes

"Machine gun rap for all my niggas in the back
Stadium packed, linebacker nigga, flash stacks
See through yellow lines
Rock a fly jersey in the summertime God
Magic marker rap, bleed Benetton
Relaxed, wrote this, comin at you crab ass culprits
Snatch ya ice off, chillin in the back, throw the lights off
Waves, water blend, rhyme flow in slow motion."

It's Yourz (Album) Wu-Tang Forever (1997).

I n my opinion, Raekwon was the best pure lyricist in Wu-Tang Clan. He recites his rhymes like an acrobat on a caffeine rush. His flow was smooth as the Nile River flowing through the hot Egypt terrain. Raekwon's lyrics are orchestrated to grab the listeners attention to focus on the complexity of what he is rapping about. I was extremely skeptical about purchasing a Raekwon solo album. I was highly disappointed when I purchased Raekwon's sophomore album "Immobilarity".

It was one of the worsts albums I ever spent money on. Regardless, the album never deterred my mind from accepting Raekwon as a first-class lyricist. There are great lyricists in the rap game that can't make a great album. Many years later I decided to purchase another Raekwon album. "Only Built 4 Cuban Linx II". Finally, I was satisfied with a Raekwon album. I was so satisfied I decided to purchase da Chef's next album "Shaolin vs. Wu-Tang".

The album made me realize why I had always been a huge fan of Raekwon. "Shaolin vs. Wu-Tang" was one of my favorite albums I purchased in that two-year time span after it was released. Raekwon is another great product from raps greatest hip hop group. A fierce flow with a barrage of machine gun lyrics, Raekwon is a top fifteen Lyrical Assassin.

12

ICE CUBE

Birth Name – O'Shea Jackson Sr.

Code Name/Moniker – Ice Cube

Albums (solo) – AmeriKKKa's Most Wanted, Kill at Will, Death Certificate, The Predator, Lethal Injection, War & Peace Vol. 1, War & Peace Vol. 2, Laugh Now, Cry Later, Raw Footage, I Am the West.

Collaboration Albums – NWA and the Posse, Straight Outta Compton, Bow Down (with Westside Connection) Terrorist Threats (with Westside Connection).

Favorite Album – Death Certificate

Top 3 Favorite Songs

1. Really Doe
2. Pushin' Weight
3. No Vaseline

Punchline Rhymes

"Thirty in a holdin tank, catch the vapors
Make me a pillow out of toilet paper
Concrete bench kickin' off the hemorrhoids;
Eses deep, don't fuck with dem boys
Phone check, collect call from the baller
Her mama said please don't call her
Do-Wah-Diddy, far from New Jack City
Seen one of my peers, "What the fuck you doin in here?"

Really Doe – (Album) Lethal Injection (1993).

Ice Cube was the vocal leader of one of the most controversial and top ten rap groups of all time NWA. Many including myself, thought Ice Cube was making a huge mistake when he made the decision to leave NWA. It turned out to be a wise decision. Ice Cube flourished as a solo artist and NWA delivered one more album before the group disbanded. Ice Cube was the explosive energy and rage of NWA. Therefore, as a solo artist he usually dominated every track with fire lyrics and the fury of a ferocious pit bull.

Cube angrily recited his lyrics with clarity, so you can fully understand exactly what Cube was conveying. Ice Cube's lyrics at times were filled with humor with street grittiness of the street lifestyle in South Central Los Angeles. Also, he was a beast when it came to diss tracks which is typical of an artist with dope lyrics. Ice Cube's first solo album "AmeriKKKa's Most Wanted" was well received by hip hop critics. The "Death Certificate" album is the album which push Cube into the arena of rap greatness.

The album included the viscous diss song "No Vaseline", a song I believe is the greatest diss song of all time. Ice Cube continued to move forward with several more highly successful solo albums. He later collaborated with W.C. and Mack-10 to form the super group Westside Connection. Ice Cube was one of the most influential lyricists on the West Coast. He is the undisputed King of the West Coast. With that said, Ice Cube is a top fifteen Lyrical Assassin.

11

COMMON

Birth Name- Lonnie Corant Jaman Shuka Rashid Lynn Jr.

Code Name/Moniker- Common Sense

Albums – Can I Borrow a Dollar?, Resurrection, One Day It'll All Make Sense, Like Water for Chocolate, Electric Circus, Be, Finding Forever, Universal Mind Control, The Dreamer/The Believer, Nobody's Smiling, Black America Again, August Green with Robert Glasper and Karriem Riggins.

Favorite Album – Be

Top 3 Favorite Songs

1. The Game
2. The Light
3. Faithful feat. Bilal & John Legend

Punchline Rhymes

"I was rollin' around, in my mind it occurred
What if God was a her?
Would I treat her the same? Would I still be runnin' game on her?
In what type of ways would I want her?
Would I want her for her mind or her heavenly body?
Couldn't be out gettin' bogus with someone so godly
If I was wit' her would I still be wantin' my ex?
The lies, the greed, the weed, the sex."

Faithful – (Album) Be (2005).

O nce again, a great emcee that had me nervous about actually spending my hard-earned money on their album. The other two were Nas and Ghostface Killah. I knew Common (or Common Sense) when he first debuted was a great emcee on his first song "Breaker 1/9." Common delivered albums after "Breaker 1/9" that I was totally not interested in listening to. At the time, I was missing out on true greatness. When I heard the song "The Light", I was shocked Common made a song I was really feeling. However, it wasn't enough for me to buy the album.

It wasn't until Kanye burst on the scene, and knowing Kanye was producing the album "Be" is when I reluctantly decided to finally buy a Common album. After listening to the album, I was blown away by Common's sharp lyrics combined with the great production of the album. The album was equipped with grade A commercial songs. Common's flow in the song "The Corner" with the Last Poets was a display of Common's superior flow and rhyme skills. Songs like "Go", "Testify", and "Faithful" was a collage of hit songs solidifying the greatness of the album.

Common didn't let up after "Be". The next album "Finding Forever" was just as great as "Be", if not better. Common completely turned up his game like a great athlete reaching his prime. The "Dreamer/ The Believer", was also a masterful work of beautiful hip hop art. Common is one of the most socially conscious rappers to ever bless the microphone. He is extremely cerebral when he formats his songs like "I Use to Love Her" and his follow up to the diss from Ice Cube "The Bitch in You." A cerebral rapper with a tremendous flow makes Common a top fifteen Lyrical Assassin.

10

GHOSTFACE KILLAH

Birth Name – Dennis Coles

Code Name/Moniker – Ghostface, Tony Starks, Ironman, Ghostdini

Albums solo – Ironman, Supreme Clientele, Bulletproof Wallets, The Pretty Toney Album, Fishscale, More Fish, The Big Doe Rehab, Ghostdini: Wizard of Poetry in Emerald City, Apollo Kids, Twelve Reasons to Die, 36 Seasons, Twelve Reasons to Die II, Supreme Clientele 2.

Collaboration Albums – Put it on Line (with Trife Diesel), Wu-Massacre (with Method Man & Raekwon), Wu-Block (with Sheek Louch), Sour Soul (with BADBADNOTGOOD), Swift and Changeable (with MF Doom as DOOMStarks), The Powers of Attraction (with Tragedy Khadafi & Killah Priest).

Favorite Album – Supreme Clientele

Top 3 Favorite Songs

1. Apollo Kids feat. Raekwon
2. Rec-room Therapy feat. Raekwon & U-God
3. Run feat. Jadakiss

Punchline Rhymes

"Check out my beaver, baby blue Glock in the safe
Seen Dorothy in the garden, gettin ski'd, row eight
We hold a belt Son, that's my word
Spot a rapper run him down, throw him out in the third
Yo check it
I think like the man behind a register
Evergreen smokin estates, Divine and Power made me treasurer."

It's Yourz (Album) Wu-Tang Forever (1997).

I t only makes sense to have a lyricist in my top ten list from the greatest rap group of all-time Wu-Tang Clan. Ghostface Killah an unparalleled product of the group with peerless advanced lyrics, had a masterful flow filled with grimy, complex New York slang. Ghostface steadily delivered a barrage of classic Wu-material laced albums. Sticking to the Wu formula, that made Wu-Tang a household name, Ghostface seemed to never disappoint. Ghostface was blessed with a unique voice, and an uncanny ability to flow using slick lyrics.

The average person needs to be a fan of Wu-Tang to understand and appreciate Ghostface's greatness. A product of a group of nine great emcees, Ghostface was able to shine with a more than productive solo career. Ghostface recited his rhymes with an up-tempo flow laced with New York City street tales. Ghost embraced the microphone with the supreme cockiness of a confident rap maestro. I wasn't sure about buying my first Ghostface album "Supreme Clientele", but after listening to it, I was filled with excitement and admiration. As a matter of fact, I was never disappointed with any of the Ghostface albums I purchased.

"The Pretty Toney Album, The Big Doe Rehab, and 12 Reasons to Die" pushed me to believe Ghostface was definitely in the upper echelon of great rap artists. Also, Ghostface's impressive body of work makes me believe he is a top ten Lyrical Assassin.

9

JAY-Z

Birth Name – Shawn Corey Carter

Code Name/Moniker – Jigga, J.Hova, Jigga Man, S. Carter

Albums (solo) – Reasonable Doubt, In My Lifetime Vol. 1, Vol. 2

...Hard Knock Life, Vol. 3...Life and Times of S.

Carter, The Dynasty Roc La Familia, The Blue

Print, The Blue Print...The Gift and the Curse,

The Black Album, Kingdom Come, American

Gangster, The Blue Print 3, Magna Carta Holy

Grail, 4:44.

Collaboration Albums – The Best of Both Worlds with R. Kelly,

Unfinished Business with R. Kelly,

Collision Course with Linkin Park,

Watch the Throne with Kanye West

Favorite Album – Vol. 3 Life and Times of S. Carter

Top 3 Favorite Songs

1. Dope Man
2. My 1st Song
3. Paper Chase feat. Foxy Brown

Punchline Rhymes

"On the canopy, my stamina be
Enough for Pamela Anderson Lee
MTV jam of the week
Made my money quick, then back to the streets
But still sittin' on blades, sippin' that Ray
Standin' on the corner of my block, hustlin'
Still gettin' that cane
Half what I paid slippin' right through customs."

> – Big Pimpin feat. Bun B & Pimp C – (Album) Vol. 3 Life
> and Times of S. Carter – (1999).

J ay-Z became the largest figure in rap, after the tragic passing of Biggie and Tupac. I don't think many people were expecting Jay-Z to seize the rap world. He did more than seize it, many people believe he became the King of New York. Jigga brought swagger he learned from the greats he hung with, to the forefront of rap consciousness. Once again some of the greats from the nineties were influenced by either Big Daddy Kane, Rakim, or Krs-One. Jay-Z was schooled well by Big Daddy Kane and like a great student he learned and mastered the art form of rap.

In 1998, Jay-Z exploded with "Vol. 2 Hard Knock Life". He capitalized on the momentum with a string of classic albums. Jay had so much success and popularity of the mainstream he started to feel himself like anyone great will. Jay-Z was dominating the late nineties and early 2000's. He clearly thought by being the King of New York, he could viciously attack Nas with "The Takeover". The Jay-Z and Nas beef in my opinion, was one of the most entertaining feuds of all time. Jay-Z gave Nas a run for his money, but the greatness of Nas prevailed.

Defeat didn't damage Jay-Z's career. He kept moving forward like a prize fighter coming back from a TKO. Jay-Z followed up with fisticuffs and uppercuts dropping one great album after another, and eventually reconciling with his nemesis. Jay-Z got better and better like a maturing fine wine. His work ethic allowed him to master his craft and develop into a top tier lyricist. Unlike the great ones before him, Jigga was able to stay relevant in the rap game for a long time. His greatness makes him a top ten Lyrical Assassin.

8

SCARFACE

Birth Name – Brad Terrence Jordan

Code Name/Moniker – Mr. Scarface, Scarface, Face Mob,

Akshen

Albums with Geto Boys- Grip It! On That Other Level, We

Can't Be Stopped, Till Death Do Us

Part, The Resurrection, Da Good da

Bad & da Ugly, The Foundation

Solo Albums- Mr. Scarface is Back, The World is

Yours, The Diary, The Untouchable,

My Homies, The Last of a Dying

Breed, The Fix, My Homies Part 2,

Made, Emeritus, Deeply Rooted,

Deeply Rooted: The Lost Files.

Collaborative Albums- The Other Side of the Law (with Facemob), One Hunid (with The Product)

Compliation Album – Deeply Rooted: The Lost Files

Favorite Album – The Untouchable

Top 3 Favorite Songs

1. On My Block
2. Mary Jane
3. Mr. Scarface is Back

Punchline Rhymes

"I'm too deep to quit, and too strict to fold

And you need to split nigga G into code
Come on, cause this year's to teach, homey speak to know it
Body bout what we talk about, you weak, you're row
The game is overcrowded so we fight for space
Neighbourhood show the hustle, still we grind to win
Tryin' to find a way, to come up on 2 pounds of yay
And double up it, ain't never happened touch it."

My Life – (Album) My Homies 2 – (1998).

S carface is the undisputed King of the South, whether he admits to it or not. Scarface has delivered one great song after another. He derived from one of the top five greatest rap groups of all time "The Geto Boys". Scarface's rough and rugged voice will immediately capture your attention. His rhymes are laced with the paranoia of a madman trying to navigate his way through a cold-hearted society. Raw, explosive, and mesmerizing all twined together sums up the Southern Rap King's methodical lyrical format.

Scarface's voice alone falls in the upper echelon of the greatest rap voices of all time. He has never failed to entertain his audience with gritty street stories of brute brutality in the urban streets. Face has consistently delivered an impressive catalog of multiple classic albums. Never venturing away from his formula, Scarface's street tales in his rhymes are legendary. Scarface was introduced to the rap world as Mr. Scarface on "The Geto Boys" debut album "Grip it! On That Other Level." Followed up by the classic "We Can't Be Stopped."

Those two albums alone made a believer out of me that Scarface would eventually develop into a superstar once his solo album released, and he didn't disappoint my expectations. "The Diary" is the album that put Scarface on a level of rap supremacy. A great voice with rough and rugged rhymes mixed with funky baseline beats and a true FOREALLA makes Scarface a top ten Lyrical Assassin.

7
TUPAC

Birth Name – Lesane Parish Crooks

Code Name/Moniker – 2Pac, Makaveli, MC New York

Albums – 2Pacalypse Now, Strictly 4 My N.I.G.G.A.Z, Me Against the World, All Eyez on Me, and The Don Killuminati: The 7 Day Theory.

Posthumous Studio Albums – R U Still Down? (Remember Me), Until the End of Tim, Better Dayz, Loyal to the Game, and Pac's Life.

Collaboration Album – Thug Life: Volume 1 (with Thug Life)

Posthumous Collaboration Album-Still I Rise (with the Outlawz)

Compliation Albums – Greatest Hits, The Rose that Grew from Concrete, Don't Go 2 Sleep, The Prophet: The Best of the Works, Nu-Mixx Klazzics, Tupac: Resurrection, 2Pac Live, The Rose, Live at the House of Blues, The Prophet Returns, Nu-Mixx Klazzics Vol. 2, Best of 2Pac Part 1: Thug, Best of 2Pac Part 2: Life, and The Lost Tapes.

Favorite Alubm – All Eyez On Me

Top 3 favorite songs

1. So Many Tears
2. Can't C Me feat. George Clinton
3. Me and My Girlfriend

Punchline Rhymes

"Now I'm lost and I'm weary, so many tears
I'm suicidal, so don't stand near me
My every move is a calculated step, to bring me closer
To embrace an early death, now there's nothin" left
There was no mercy on the streets, I couldn't rest
I'm barely standin', bout to go to pieces, screamin' peace
And though my soul was deleted, I couldn't see it
I had my mind full of demons tryin' to break free."

So Many Tears – (Album) Me Against the World – (1995).

T upac Shakur is the greatest rap icon to ever bless the microphone. His iconic status overshadows his accomplishments as a great rapper. Tupac is a descendant of a Black Panther mother and father. His mother Afeni, was a part of the largest trial of New York at the time the Panther 21 while pregnant with Tupac. Greatness was his destiny. However, his rise to stardom was not an easy journey.

He was destined to be a warrior of black righteousness. Tupac Shakur was a man of many talents with an impeccable work ethic. A workaholic and genius embedded together only equals greatness. After watching the movie Juice, someone told me the person playing the crazy role of Bishop was a rapper. I never knew Bishop from the movie Juice would turn out to be raps elite.

Tupac was raised by his mother to be an intellectual with a rebellious nature toward an injustice system of racism. Early in his career, Tupac's lyrics were filled with social consciousness reaching deep into the depths of the horrors of poverty in urban poverty-stricken environments. Tupac's voice was filled with the rage of a person who wanted to dig deep inside your soul and feel the pain of what he was conveying. After his brief prison stint, Tupac's rhymes became laced with more venom of street life and personal pain.

Musically, Tupac was on the level of Michael Jackson, Madonna, Prince, and Elvis Pressley. From the time the double disc "All Eyez on Me" and "Makavelli" dropped, Tupac was on the level of supreme music superiority. Tupac was prematurely taken away from the world, his family, and his fans, but before he left us he had cemented his mark in the rap game. The greatest rap icon of all time. Tupac Shakur is definitely a top ten Lyrical Assassin.

6

THE

NOTORIOUS

B.I.G.

Birth Name – Christopher George Latore Wallace

Code Name/Moniker – Biggie Smalls, Biggie, Frank White,

Big Poppa

Albums – Ready to Die, Life After Death

The King & I (with Faith Evans)

Favorite Album – Life After Death – 1997

Top 3 Favorite Songs

1. I Got a Story to Tell
2. My Downfall feat. DMC
3. Ready to Die

Punchline Rhymes

"Uhh, I dream filthy
My moms and pops mixed me with Jamaican Rum and Whiskey
Huh, what a set up
Shoulda pushed 'em dead off, wipe the sweat off
'Cause in this world I'm dead off, squeeze lead off
Benz sped off, ain't no shook hands in Brook-land
Army fatigue break up teams, the enemies
Look man, you want to see me locked up, shot up."

           – My Downfall (Album) Life After Death (1997).

T he enormity of what happened to Biggie & Tupac left a depressing sadness on hip hop for many years. Biggie Smalls may he rest in peace, died way before his time. Unlike his friend and foe Tupac, Biggie only released two albums before he was tragically taken away from the world. Don't get me wrong, I was definitely a fan of Biggie, but at the time I wasn't considering Biggie as the greatest of all time. Honestly, a few years after Biggie passed away there was a New York propaganda machine hyping Biggie as the best of all time that left me wildly confused.

After a passage of time, I believe if Biggie would have put out at least two more albums he would have rightfully been crowned the greatest of all time. 1988 and 1994 were considered the Golden Years of Hip Hop. West Coast rap was dominating the air waves in the early nineties, mainly due to gangster rap being more relevant to black people nationwide. In the early nineties, if you were not from New York it was hard trying to comprehend what New York rappers were rapping about.

Many critics believed Biggie saved the East Coast, I believe it was Biggie along with Wu-Tang Clan that saved the East Coast, with Biggie being the largest, figuratively and lyrically. Biggie was the king of New York. Biggie, raised in Brooklyn, was influence by Big Daddy Kane another Brooklynite. Biggie was lyrically inclined with great rhythm to his flow. Biggie had no problem telling you how fat, black, and ugly he was, but he would tell you he was a player with nothing but style.

Biggie courageously possessed an aura of self-esteem that had every obese, unattractive guy in the world feeling damn good about himself as long as their game and clothes are correct. Biggie was so masterful with his flow he was even able to change his flow for the song "Notorious Thugs" featuring Bone-Thugs-N-Harmony, which was a genius-like feat at the time. Once again, Biggie was taken away from the world far to early leaving fans starve for more of his greatness. The Notorious B.I.G. is a top ten lyrical assassin.

5

RAKIM

Birth Name – William Michael Griffin Jr.

Code Name/Moniker – Rakim Allah, The God MC, Kid Wizard

Albums – as Eric B. & Rakim

Paid In Full, Follow the Leader, Let the Rhythm Hit Em Don't Sweat the Technique

Solo Albums – The 18th Letter, The Master, The Seventh Seal

Compliation Albums – Classic, Gold, The Archive= Live, Lost &

Found

Favorite Album – Follow the Leader

Top 3 Favorite Songs

1. Paid in Full
2. Follow the Leader
3. Mahogany

Punchline Rhymes

"When people see me stop and ask me when the album droppin'
The wait is over, information like a soldier
Like I told ya, greater stronger, now that I'm older

I broke the, code of silence with overloads of talents
My only challenge, is not to explode in violence
I'm Asiatic, and blazin' microphones a habit
At least once durin' the course of a day, it's automatic

In ghetto apparel, mind of a Egyptian Pharaoh."

– It's Been a Long Tim (Album) The 18th Letter-1997

A former saxophone player, Rakim's flow was comparable to a laid-back jazz musician. Smooth, silky, and suave. I will have to embarrassedly admit I wasn't a fan of Rakim when I first heard him rap. I was bored and disinterested. I soon learned, I wasn't lyrically intellectual enough to appreciate Rakim's style. Once I became a believer, I was awed by the sophistication of Rakim's technique. Rakim the ultimate rhyme slayer possessed a voice full of soul while he smoothly recited his intricate rhymes.

Rakim, derived from the first era of the golden years of rap, where his rhyme styles separated him from the rest of the pack. Rakim was properly dubbed as the God Emcee due to his complex rhyme patterns that were far more advanced than his peers. Just like KRS-One represents knowledge, Chuck D represents the voice, Big Daddy Kane represents rhymes, Rakim represents superior rhyme technique. Rakim's style made many New York rappers re-think how to deliver their respective rhymes. He raised the bar in the rap game and architected a blue print for complex rhyme craftmanship. Rakim fathered sophisticated rhyme styles and only the truly great emcees in years to come were able to emulate his flow. His lyrical superiority is coveted mostly by hardcore rhyme fanatic hip hop fans. In my opinion, Rakim is a top five Lyrical Assassin.

4

CHUCK D

Birth Name – Carlton Douglas Ridenhour

Code Name/Moniker – Carl Ryder, The Hard Rhymer, The

Rhyme Animal, Lyrical Assassin,

Mistachuck

Albums – with Public Enemy

Yo! Bum Rush the Show, It Takes a Nation of Millions

To Hold Us Back, Fear of a Black Planet, Apocalypse

91....The Enemy Strikes Black, Muse Sick-N-Hour

Mess Age, He Got Game, There's a Poison Goin' On,

Revolrertrution, New Whirl Odor, How You Sell Soul to

A Souless People Who Sold Their Soul?, Most of My

Heroes Still Don't Appear on No Stamp, The Evil

Empire of Everything, Man Plans God Laughs

Solo Albums – Autobiography of Mistachuck, The Black in Man,

If I Can't Change the People Around Me I

Charge the People Around Me

Favorite Album- It Takes a Nation of Millions to Hold Us Back

Top 3 Favorite Songs

1. Black Steel in the Hour of Chaos
2. Welcome to the Terrordome
3. Can't Truss It

Punchline Rhymes

"I got so much trouble on my mind
Refuse to lose
Here's your ticket
Hear the drummer get wicked
The crew to you to push the back to Black
Attack so I sack and jack
Then slapped the Mac
Now I'm ready to mic it."

Welcome to the Terrordome –(Album) Fear of a Black
Planet – (1989).

Chuck D hands down had the most powerful voice hip hop has ever heard. His delivers his rhymes like he is thrusting every word down your throat with the force of supreme horsepower. Chuck D the front man for the political minded super rap group Public Enemy captured your attention with every line he aggressively recites. In his prime, he was like the Malcolm X of rap music. He made you feel the energy as if Malcolm X or MLK was speaking. Chuck D opened the simple minds of youths in America in the late eighties with an explosion of political base rhymes.

Just like KRS-One, Chuck D was also a teacher. A teacher of injustices of melanin people, who learned from Chuck that the system was not on their side. He definitely opened my mind in high school when I didn't have a clue of what I was going to have to deal with as a black man in American society. Chuck D forced the older generation to at least listen to a music that they felt was a bunch of jib jab and noise. His rhymes were laced with the venom of social consciousness that was embraced universally. Decades later, I can still hear Chuck D's powerful voice telling me "he got a letter from the government" or "Brothers gonna work it out."

Those rhymes help me navigate my way through my late teens as a young military serviceman. Chuck D was one rapper, I believe, that should have replaced the Al Sharpton's and Jesse Jackson's of the world and became a leader and voice for the people. Chuck D wasn't only a Lyrical Assassin as he dubbed himself on the credits of Public Enemy's third album "Fear of a Black Planet." He was also a prophet delivering jaw dropping knowledge just like Malcolm and Farrakhan. His rhymes were exactly what young men yearning for maturity needed to hear. Chuck D had millions of young black men world-wide feeling dam good about being black. In my opinion, Chuck D is a top five Lyrical Assassin.

3

KRS-ONE

Birth Name – Lawrence Parker

Code Name/Moniker- The Teacha, Knowledge Reigns Supreme

Over Nearly Everyone, The Blastmaster

Albums – With Boogie Down Productions – Criminal Minded, By

Any Means Necessary, Ghetto Music: The Blueprint of

Hip Hop, Edutainment, Live Hardcore Worldwide, Sex

And Violence.

Solo Albums – as KRS-One – Return of the Boom Rap, KRS-

One, I Got Next, The Sneak Attack, Spiritual

Minded, Kristyles, Keep Right, Life, Adventures in

Emceein, Maximum Strength, The BDP Album,

Now Hear This, and The World is Mine.

Favorite Album – Sex and Violence

Top 3 Favorite Songs

1. My Philosophy
2. Poisonous Products
3. 100 Guns

Punchline Rhymes

"That's worse than always talking about sex, let's build
It ain't enough to study Clarence 13X
The white man ain't the devil I promise
You want to see the devil take a look at Clarence Thomas
Now you're saying, "Who?" like you a owl
Throw in the towel, the devil is Colin Powell
You talk about being African and being black
Colin Powell's black, but Libya he'll attack." –

Build and Destroy (Album) Sex and Violence –(1992).

The Teacher, The Blastmaster, Knowledge Reigns Supreme Over Nearly Everyone is the rap voice of knowledge, knowledge, and more knowledge. There would be no other emcee you can find more intellectual than KRS-One. The front member for the super political group Boogie Down Productions. KRS-One made political rap very popular in the late eighties. His rhymes made high school kids like myself conscious about the government, poverty, and all the ills of society that was relevant to black people in America.

KRS-One was rightfully dubbed as the teacher. He shared knowledge about ancient Egypt, the bible, religion, drug dealing, community organization, economic empowerment, and the typical trappings related to living in an impoverish environment. KRS-One teachings informed young black youth about topics the American school system curriculum wouldn't dare teach young black kids.

KRS-One was influential early in his career in battle rapping and diss records with his historical battle against MC Shan and the legendary Juice Crew. Even though Boogie Down Productions was considered a rap group, KRS-One was the leading voice of the group. Over the years, the group membership interchanged several times. First, when DJ Scott LaRock was murdered after BDP's first album Criminal Minded was released. BDP continued to push forward with a total of five albums, before KRS-One decided to go solo under his name.

The Blastmaster KRS-One would often create a song and capture your full attention with content you never thought much about. Songs like "Black Cop" depicts the beginnings of the Black Cop in America. The song illustrates how Black Cops are not too distant in time from being the subject of police brutality and how they will inadvertently use the same tactics of violence on those who reign from the same communities the cops grew up in. A song like "Beef" will educate you about the mental distress cows go through prior to being slaughtered and how eating the butchered animals will translate the stress to your mind, body, and soul.

KRS-One will either teach you something or reiterate something to you that you already knew but didn't give much thought to. No matter what the situation maybe, KRS-One will give you something to think about and make it entertaining, like BDP's appropriately named fourth album "Edutainment" meaning education plus entertainment. The son of a Jamaican mother, KRS-One often used a Jamaican style flavor in the reflection of his voice. Every time I purchased a BDP, or KRS-One album I knew I was going to learn something interesting that would cause me to further investigate.

I recently witness KRS-One perform live and the show blew me away after all these years. KRS-One is definitely a top three Lyrical Assassin prophet emcee.

2

BIG DADDY KANE

Birth Name – Antonio Hardy

Code Name/Monikers – Baby Dayliner, Blackanova

Albums – Long Live the Kane, It's a Big Daddy Thing, Taste of Chocolate, Prince of Darkness, Looks Like a Job For…, Daddy's Home, Veteranz' Day

Top 3 Favorite Songs

1. Warm It Up Kane
2. Young, Gifted, and Black
3. Set It Off

Punchline Rhymes

"When I'm ridin' in my Volvo, cops harass me
They never ride past me, they hound me like Lassie
Wantin' to give me a summons or a ticket
Huh, I got a place for them to stick it (kick it)
They can't understand to see a black man
Drivin' a car that costs 25 grand
The first thing they say is "Where'd you steal her?"
And then they assume that I'm a drug dealer."

Another Victory – (Album) It's A Big Daddy Thing – (1989).

Decades before anyone was using the word swagger, before Dapper Rappers like Biggie, Tupac, Cam'ron, Kanye, Big Sean, Jay-Z, and even Puff Daddy it was Big Daddy Kane that designed the blueprint for swag. KANE meaning King Asiatic Nobody's Equal had two switches with his rap delivery, suave and fiery. No one could out dress BDK, and he had arguably the most hype, dope, sweetest, smoothest, and creative rhymes of anyone in the rap game then and now. Big Daddy Kane was a member of the legendary Juice Crew. Also, he derived from the Golden Era when rappers started to outshine the dee jays with superior lyrics.

BDK rhymes influenced future super stars. His influence schooled some of the greatest lyricists of all time such as Biggie and Jay-Z. If you listen closely to Biggie and Jay-Z's rhymes, it has BDK written all over them. Big Daddy Kane had a smooth flow when flowing first became popularized in the rap game. BDK was the guy who would show up to a battle an out dress you and out rhyme you.

Big Daddy was extremely versatile making a song "Who Am I" with Gamilah Shabazz the daughter of Malcolm X, who did a nice job rapping on the song. Personally, I wish Kane would have stuck with the formula that made him a great emcee. Unfortunately, Kane got carried away with being a lady's man, and a fashion icon. Review the album and the cover of his fourth album "Prince of Darkness." Also, he posed nude in a magazine with Madonna which solidified him as a lady's man. With all the extracurricular activity, Kane eventually started to stray away from street lyrics. Big Daddy made songs with R&B stars such as Barry White, Alyson Williams, and Barbara Weathers. It doesn't matter, BDK had already cemented his legacy as an upper echelon, dapper rapper who became a trend setter. Big Daddy Kane is a top two Lyrical Assassin.

1

NAS

Birth Name- Nasir Bin Olu Dara Jones

Code Names/Moniker – Nasty Nas, Nas Escobar

Albums– Illmatic, It Was Written, I Am, Nastradamus, Stillmatic, God's Son, The Lost Tapes, Street's Disciples, Hip Hop Is Dead, Untitled "N*****", Life Is Good, NASIR.

Collaboration Albums – The Firm: The Album (with the Firm),

Nas & Ill Will Records Presents QB's

Finest, Distant Relatives (with Damian

Marley).

Favorite Album – Stillmatic

Top 3 favorite songs

1. If I Ruled the World feat. Lauryn Hill
2. Get Down
3. Street Disciple feat. Olu Dara

Punchline Rhymes

"By the time of age nine I'm already decidin'
If I can protect mommy from the hood by fightin'
Or usin' a knife or a gun when I'm twenty-one
By then them hoods woulda pushed their way in our apartment
And we die then, so I been a young nervous wreck in the projects
Watchin' them older niggaz pass pot and they high man
I'm just a young boy, snot nose, hair nappy
Cops ride by squeezin' their trigger fingers at me."

Reasons –(Album) Street Disciples- (2004).

Nas's debut album "Illmatic" was considered a masterpiece when it was released in 1994. I will admit, I was more of a fan of East Coast rap, but honestly the East Coast had lost a lot of its momentum to the West Coast at the time. However, when "The World is Yours" dropped I was definitely feeling the new kid on the block, Nas. It wasn't enough for me to buy the album, so I slept on a great album like many others due to the lack of sales.

When Nas's sophomore album dropped "It Was Written" the song "If I ruled the World" feat. Lauryn Hill, a remake of Kurtis Blow's "If I ruled the World" was another great gem by Nas along with the video. For some strange reason it still wasn't enough for me to buy the album. It wasn't until I heard "Ether" on Nas's fifth album "Stillmatic" is when I decided to buy my first Nas album. After listening to "Stillmatic Freestlye" prior to Stillmatic and Ether dropping, I was convinced Nas was a top- notch lyricist.

After listening to the album Stillmatic, I was further convinced Nas was one of the greatest. Nas proved to me not only was he an upper echelon lyricist, he was nobody to try to punk on a diss track. Nas is a cerebral lyricist who drops knowledge about black history, injustices, and the realities of the streets of the black ghettos in America. Is it fair to say Nas can be inconsistent with what he is feeling at the moment like using the moniker Nas Escobar? Yes, Also, Nas has been inconsistent with selecting the best beats for his songs that can be a waste of his great lyrics. Currently the Nas catalog runs deep with one classic song after another. Nas has songs not many people paid much attention to that were great songs like "Reasons" "The Rest of My Life" and "The Cross".

Nas like a true genius he is, destroyed the racist Fox News network with slick words to describe the powers of the race baiting devilish news channel. Phrases like "digital devil", "visual cancer", and "idiot box". Nas brilliantly attacked Bill O'Reilly who has since resigned and the rest of the liberal hating network with the song "Sly Fox".

KRS-One provided knowledge, Big Daddy Kane provided rhymes, & Rakim provided an advance rhyme technique. The three great ones before him designed the blueprint for Nas to follow. However, Nas learned to be a master of all three of those elements. The versatility of Nas is what separates him from the rest. Unlike many of the great ones before him, Nas was able to stay relevant and he continued to be enamored by his fan base for many years since his debut album Illmatic. In my opinion, Nas is the greatest Lyrical Assassin of all time.

HONORABLE
MENTIONS

- Kool Mo Dee – How You Like Me Now
- YoYo- You Can't Play With My YoYo
- Sir-Mix-A-Lot – Beepers
- RZA – Good Night
- Ol' Dirty Bastard – Brooklyn Zoo
- Kwame – Only You
- MC Serch – Here It Comes
- Lil Kim – Lighters Up
- Freddie Gibbs – Deeper
- Ice-T – The Tower
- Beanie Sigel – Feel It in the Air
- Styles P – I Get High
- The Nine – Whatcha Want?
- Mack 10 – Foe Life
- Boss – Recipe of a Hoe
- Bubba Sparxxx – Deliverance
- Ron C- Funky Lyrics
- Bust Down – Putcha Bally's On
- Mystikal- Here I Go
- Master P- Bout It, Bout It
- Doug E. Fresh – The Show
- GZA – Breaker, Breaker
- DJ Quik – Tonight
- Method Man- Bring the Pain
- Havoc – Tell Me to My Face

- Kodak Black – Skirt
- MC Breed – Ain't No Future in Your Frontin'
- MC Eiht – Straight Up Menace
- Ja Rule- New York
- Lauryn Hill – Doo Wop That Thing
- Kool G. Rap – Ill Street Blues
- Brother Ali – Uncle Sam Goddamn
- Donny Cashflow – Purple
- Don P.- Chico Montana
- Black Rob – Whoa
- Trick Daddy – I'm a Thug
- Mia X- The Party Don't Stop
- C.L. Smooth – T.R.O.Y
- Biz Markie- Spring Again
- Eve – Love is Blind
- Juvenile – Rodeo
- Willie D – Coon
- Da Brat – Give it to You

TOP 50 RAP GROUPS/DUOS

(1) Wu-Tang Clan
(2) Public Enemy
(3) Boogie Down Productions
(4) NWA
(5) Geto Boys
(6) A Tribe Called Quest
(7) Outkast
(8) De La Soul
(9) Run DMC
(10) Mobb Deep
(11) Bone-Thugs-N-Harmony
(12) Gang Starr
(13) Nice & Smooth
(14) EPMD
(15) The Fat Boys
(16) Naughty by Nature
(17) Salt & Pepa
(18) Brand Nubian
(19) Grand Master Flash & The Furious Five
(20) Poor Righteous Teachers
(21) 3rd Bass
(22) The Click
(23) Das Efx
(24) Digital Underground
(25) Lords of the Underground

(26) Beastie Boys

(27) The Coup

(28) Goodie Mob

(29) Kriss Kross

(30) The LOX

(31) Top Authority

(32) Whodini

(33) Pete Rock and C.L. Smooth

(34) Fu-Schnickens

(35) Souls of Mischief

(36) The Roots

(37) Arrested Development

(38) Slaughterhouse

(39) Capone-N-Noreaga

(40) Do or Die

(41) Black Sheep

(42) Three 6 Mafia

(43) TRU

(44) UTFO

(45) Digable Planets

(46) The Lost Boys

(47) Black Moon

(48) Above the Law

(49) The Five Footaz

(50) Da Youngsta's

Printed in the United States
By Bookmasters